The Enchanted Self

New Directions in Therapeutic Intervention

A series edited by *Marti T. Loring*, The Center for Mental Health and Human Development, and The Emotional Abuse Institute, Atlanta, Georgia

This book is part of a series. The publisher will accept continuation orders which may be cancelled at any time and which provide for automatic billing and shipping of each title in the series upon publication. Please write for details.

The Enchanted Self
A Positive Therapy

Barbara Becker Holstein

harwood academic publishers
Australia • Canada • China • France • Germany • India • Japan •
Luxembourg • Malaysia • The Netherlands • Russia • Singapore •
Switzerland • Thailand • United Kingdom

Amsteldijk 166
1st Floor
1079 LH Amsterdam
The Netherlands

Cover: *THE ENCHANTED SELF*® muse represents the higher self. The hand mirror suggests deep introspection, but our muse holds the Earth casually because she knows that life and the world should not be taken too seriously. The flowering tree implies renewal and creativity and the vase under her left arm represents the mind as a vessel. The symbol derives from the medieval notion of bodily humors and the alchemist's precept: "That which does not mix well, dies."

THE ENCHANTED SELF® is a registered trademark of Barbara Becker Holstein.

British Library Cataloguing in Publication Data

Holstein, Barbara Becker
    The enchanted self : a positive therapy. – (New directions
    in therapeutic intervention ; v. 1)
    1. Psychotherapy   2. Memory
    I. Title
    616.8'914

ISBN 90-5702-503-5

To humanity

And then the lightness came
Filling all the places
That darkness had bound.
And there was brightness
And joy going all
Around!
For each person
Enchantment found

— *Barbara Becker Holstein*

Contents

Introduction
to the Series

New Directions in Therapeutic Intervention is designed as a vehicle for the expression of innovative visions in the area of therapeutic intervention. Individual titles will examine the needs of special client populations and describe creative helping strategies within a theoretical context. The editor's hopes are twofold: That this series will serve as a collection of well-defined maps to guide caring professionals in their helping journey, and that it will provide new ideas and a sense of hope for intervention with individuals who, isolated and in emotional pain, reach out for connection with others in their human family.

Preface

In my years as a psychologist, I have come to believe that most people seeking psychotherapy are unhappy not only because of earlier hurts and traumas — as well as present frustrations and problems — but because they cannot access earlier happy moments often enough, resulting in not being able to experience enough positive states of well-being. Much contemporary psychotherapy, no matter how well-intended and deliberate, often minimizes the accessing of earlier states of well-being and the joys associated with them. After all, we are trained as therapists to look for dysfunction rather than function. This training can result in our not sufficiently recognizing talents, potentials, and capacities for joy within our clients. This book is intended to help you as a mental health professional — including those of you at the para professional levels of training — as well as allied professionals such as educators and nurses, learn how to help your patients, clients, or students access those earlier states of well-being unique to each individual. It is also intended to help you — whether you are a clinician or other interested party, perhaps the woman or man who may have been in therapy yet still wonders why he or she does not feel whole — learn how to better access your positive states of well-being so that you too may experience more joy and fulfillment in you own life. It is these unique states of well-being that I have come to label *THE ENCHANTED SELF*®.

Exactly what is THE ENCHANTED SELF? A complete explanation of each of the concepts mentioned here can be found on page 183. It is nothing less than the capacity to reclaim, reintegrate, or adapt positive states of being from previous times in our lives into present-day workable, pleasurable, growth-promoting, joyful states of being. I call the actual positive states that are retrieved Positive Fingerprints of the Mind, Positive Fingerprints of the Body, and Shadow Prints. These are the various Enchanted Memories within every person, unique and distinct for each of us. Each is as individual as our fingerprints. And, just as we each have ten fingers and, therefore, ten fingerprints, we have many Enchanted Memories, each generating different positive capacities within us.

Positive Fingerprints of the Mind are positive conscious memories of actual happenings or mental imaginations and the feelings associated with them.

Positive Fingerprints of the Body are enhanced memories retrieved through the body.

Shadow Prints of the Mind are memories not tied to specific cognitions, that emerge in the retrieval process. At times they are not associated with language, but with smells or other sensations. Shadow Prints can be important in the emergence of THE ENCHANTED SELF, as they often contain positive feelings such as: peacefulness, relaxation, authenticity, connectedness, wholeness, and integrity. Mystical and spiritual feelings are also Shadow Prints.

All these retrieved states fluctuate and change over a lifetime. At various times in one's life, one may utilize different combinations of positive memories to achieve sublime states of being. That which pleases us and moves us to joy at age twenty-five may not do so at age sixty-five. Our talents and capacity to activate certain talents may change over the years, so that our achieved positive states of being ebb and flow rather than staying fixed.

Each of us has an Enchanted Self capacity which can be trained and utilized, again and again, all during life. The more we practice retrieval of positive memory traces, both in the mind and body, the more we develop the self-esteem necessary to feel entitled to positive states of being; the more we learn how to get our needs met so we can succeed in sustaining positive states of being; the more the capacity to do so becomes automatic; and the more we experience our Enchanted Self. As in any other form of learning, repetition and practice are essential.

Each of us is unique and profoundly beautiful. A Jewish silent prayer is written: "Thank you, God, for letting me be born with my uniqueness and special gifts because if there had already been someone exactly like me, I would not need to have been born."[1]

As we are able to recognize and fully appreciate our Enchanted Self, a wondrous central enchanted core emerges. I have labeled this core The Song of the Soul. This is the most authentic sense of one's self that we can contact within us, based on unique perceptions, attributes and talents, and sense of purpose. In order to achieve a full appreciation for The Song of the Soul, we must be able to sort through and discard the dysfunction and mislabeling that hover, casting shadows around our talents and early wishes. These arise from others' expectations, humiliating labels, dysfunctional family patterns, and destructive societal expectations.

As a song can be played or sung in a thousand ways, one's Enchanted Self can have many verses and, as I have indicated, may be experienced differently at various stages of life.

While it is not easy to access one's Song of the Soul, it is quite easy to document and separate out what is positive about a particular person, be it your client or yourself, from what is dysfunctional and negative. In our competitive society, we have a tendency to discard, dismiss, or diminish one another. Sometimes we do this by permanently placing people in pigeonholes; at other times we are much more subtle. Often, therapy ends with both client and therapist having agreed to pigeonhole the client in certain ways that mislabel her, leaving her unable to "soar" even though technically she may function "better."

Everyone has an Enchanted Self capacity. Fortunately, within all of us there are many Positive Fingerprints of the Mind and Body, as well as Shadow Prints. Fortunately, too, the Song of the Soul is so fluid and flexible that it can be played with a harp or a drum. Once you understand the process of retrieval, you will be able to retrieve Positive Fingerprints of the Mind and Shadow Prints of the Mind leading to the experience of your Enchanted Self. Some of you may also find your Song of the Soul; others may not, without the care and assistance of a trained professional to help you, or more practice based on the exercises in this book.

As you read, you will have an opportunity, via such directed exercises, to see how it feels to be in touch with your own Enchantment. You will have a chance to retrieve Positive Fingerprints of the Mind and Shadow Prints. You will be able to practice discovering and validating your talents, strengths, and potential.

As a therapist myself, I am in no way discarding or diminishing the role of the therapist or the allied professional. Rather, I am attempting to make a needed correction. THE ENCHANTED SELF as a paradigm shift and technique can be a powerful tool for increasing a client's sense of well-being.

This is an opportunity to make an improvement in the mental health care given in the Western world, care that often focuses on pathology rather than wellness.

Most of us in the mental health field realize how profoundly damaging many Western values are for everyone in our society. We live in a competitive society which has defined as "superior" those values associated with positively valued traits for males: aggressiveness, public success, winning, or control of those "under" them. Those who do not "win" in these terms are perceived as less valuable, less whole, less important men or women. As a result, many people become dismissive of capacities that otherwise might provide contentment and joy but do not provide prestige or great financial rewards.

These are the very people who come into our treatment rooms — often women who lead domestic lives that may be judged unremarkable by many. Even those judged "successful" in our competitive society often dismiss or fail to acknowledge the parts of themselves that give them the most pleasure or joy but are not related to achievement in their careers.

This situation is complicated even further when many therapists, themselves, are dismissive of the pleasures of domestic or creative life. They, too, may suffer from placing too much emphasis on the various competitive urges and strivings which have taken them through graduate training but also have blinded them to the more natural, simple, integrative experiences of life. Certainly there are therapists who are not only overachievers from dysfunctional families, but who may push through adult life running from their own depressive tendencies![2]

As we move into THE ENCHANTED SELF together, I want you to know firsthand of my journey of Enchantment, both as a professional and private person. I hope my self-revelations will encourage you to undertake your journey of personal Enchantment as you learn more about THE ENCHANTED SELF, whether your ultimate goal is to provide better mental health care or whether you are looking for a path that will permit you to continue your own self-repair and growth. I hope that the following pages will guide you, whether you journey on your own or choose a sympathetic professional helper.

For more information, or if you would like to receive *THE
ENCHANTED SELF*® newsletter, please write to: *THE
ENCHANTED SELF*, P.O. Box 2112, Ocean, New Jersey 07712.
If you wish to communicate directly with me via e-mail, write to
ENCSELF@AOL. COM. Also, visit my web site at
http://www.enchantedself.com/

Acknowledgments

There are so many people, literally hundreds, who have encouraged and given me assistance along the way. It's impossible to note everyone but let me say thank you to the following.

To my husband Dr. Russell M. Holstein, I thank you for support on every level — emotional, spiritual, and financial. Without the quality of connection that our marriage offers, I would not have had the time or psychic energy to write this book! I acknowledge my children Jessica and Justin for your support, good humor, love, and encouragement.

I am grateful to Betty Wainright, our office secretary, for her helpfulness and unrelenting support of my work. I thank Sandi Horwitz, who worked with me in the earliest days of conceptualizing THE ENCHANTED SELF; her expertise as a professional writer and editor was invaluable. Thanks go also to Carin MacPherson, who came in on the scene just in time to help with the typing and retyping of chapters; her enthusiasm and energy were deeply appreciated. I acknowledge Elizabeth Friar Williams, psychotherapist, writer, and editor, who gave invaluable editorial advice. My heartfelt thanks to editor Kathleen O'Malley, who helped conceptualize and encouraged this book.

My thanks to Doreen Laperdon-Addison, a friend and collaborator whose devotion to the concept and willingness to process ideas profoundly strengthened me. My friends Dr. Sandra Prince-Embury and Dr. Barbara Fleisher encouraged me to venture forth and write in my own style; and Felicia Weinberg patiently helped me proofread. I am indebted to Barbara Knight, my movement alignment teacher, and Cynthia Costa, my fitness instructor, for constant support in strengthening my body, as well as encouraging my work.

Prologue

And there came a time when my spirit seemed broken …
 but the music played on
And not all at once, rather little by little, I was mended.
At the same time I took an old dream I had lain to rest
from out of a deep and hidden place, and I gave it new Life.
I took my dream on as my own and gave it ounces of
 courage I didn't know I had.
Not understanding the point or path,
I knew my pursuit right as it filled me with
 Such Passion
And connected me to myself.
We need to give Life to our Dreams
 Else the Soul's Wing
 Stay Broken …

— Sori Gottdenker, poet

As you read these pages, you will get to know me along with people who have come into my life. I have tried to share my true impressions and feelings at the time, even if painful. Yet there is no one mentioned in this book to whom I am not grateful for having been part of my journey in life.

To my therapists, I would like to mention that if therapy had gone without flaw, if I had never experienced minor violations, I would not have been able to discuss my insights based on the delicate balance between client and therapist — particularly when the client experiences minor, often overlooked, violations.

To my parents, I wish to say thank you for always loving me so completely and devotedly. Your graceful humanity has permitted both of you to age with wisdom and humor, staying not only deeply in love but having the capacities to resolve and work through virtually all the difficult issues I perceived in childhood. It makes me hopeful about my own life and human capacities to have seen so much growth and positive love reflected in my childhood home.

To my immediate family, I wish to thank all of you for the rich-
ness of the life–fabric that includes memories, history, genetic
makeup, and hopes, dreams, and lessons learned from all of you. To
my mother's mother, I add a special thanks for having shared with
me her love of culture and a sense of the artistic, whether it was
through listening to Caruso records on the wind-up Victrola™,
showing me her beautiful colored glass plates, or letting me "make
up" music on her upright piano. Even though I grieve because her
true Enchantment did not emerge in daily life, I thank her for the
kernels of wisdom regarding an enhanced life which at some profound level she knew and was able to transmit to me.

To my other relatives, I hope my disguises were sufficient that you
do not clearly identify yourselves. Be certain that my feelings of connection to all my extended family, those still with me as well as those
deceased, far outweigh any of the conflictual childhood feelings
expressed in this book. I hope that you, along with my therapists,
realize that if my childhood had been blissful and without inner struggle, this material could never have emerged as instructive for so many.

To my clients, I thank you for permitting me the privilege of
accompanying you on your sacred journeys of development. I
cannot imagine my own growth having come this far without the
opportunity you provided to share aspects of your pain and joy. I
hope your stories serve as messengers of hope to many others.[3]

To the women I originally interviewed who gave me the gift of
discovering that the joy in people's lives often outweighs dysfunction, I thank you. Your candor, honesty, and willingness to share so
much about your lives with me was not only helpful in the restoration of my own sense of self but gave me the thrust to write this
book. Although I could not tell all of your stories, I treasure them
deeply.[4]

We are all entitled to our Enchanted Selves. By that I mean we are
all entitled to find ways to bring forth into adulthood our talents,
preferences, strengths, and potentials.

Let me end with a little fairy tale:

Once upon a time there was a princess who set out on a raft to find the
Enchanted Forest. She took with her a canteen full of hopes and dreams,
minimal emotional provisions, and outdated maps. Soon the raft swayed. At

times she was almost swept overboard. Finally she arrived at what she thought was the Enchanted Forest only to discover that it was no longer Enchanted!

Whether we are "princesses" or "princes," each of us sets out on our raft hoping to come ashore at the Enchanted Forest. Most of us find that our canteens full of hopes and dreams, our minimal emotional provisions, and outdated maps are usually not enough. When we get to the other side, we find that indeed there is no easy Enchantment. Often we stumble and fall. Some of us get very bruised. Some of us struggle to another shore. Some of us stay. But at some level we learn that the forest is not Enchanted. Yet, we also learn that there is Enchantment. This Enchantment is not within the hoped-for Enchanted Forest but within ourselves, our Enchanted Selves. That is what you will be learning more about as you journey with me through the following pages.

Chapter One

Beginning the Journey

S EVEN years ago, after many years in private practice, combined with a lifetime experiencing the complicated role of being female in our society, I decided that I wanted to know more about women's development, via a case study approach. I wanted a first-hand sense of what women would tell me about how they perceived girlhood messages. I wished to hear for myself how these messages had impacted on the ordinary woman's sense of self and her development. How do the messages that girls receive about what they should become interface with a woman's sense of selfhood?

Many of my clients, as well as I myself, had experienced violation in terms of childhood messages. Although women had talked to me about having a special place, a sacred place where one could feel whole, this space was often violated and shattered by various forms of victimization. How many women have been told such things as, "Don't worry about a career, just worry about finding a husband" or, "There is only enough money for one of you to go to college so it will be your brother." I too had suffered from negative messages which did not help me thrive. As a teenager in the late fifties I clearly understood society's message that I needed to be pretty, act dumb but flirtatious and appealing, and find a husband by my senior

1

year of college. Even though my parents supported my intellectual growth, society along with my extended family's other messages had tremendous impact on my development.

I realize of course that men, as well as women, can be profoundly violated by our society and/or family expectations, by the demands and artificial standards which have been set for them. They too can feel the loss of self just as I and my women clients seemed to have felt a loss. However, for me at the time, my greatest urge was to better understand the pain that women experience when given negative messages in childhood that hurt their flowering. As a woman my yearning was to research women, with whom I felt a strong connection emotionally and biologically. I also knew that little research had been done on female adult development. To conduct my research I developed a structured interview which I administered to 18 non-client women, ranging in age from 35 to their early 80's. Some had had psychotherapy, most had not. The women were white, upper to middle class, primarily from the East Coast of the United States but one woman resided in Europe. My questions covered messages as well as interpersonal conditions of the women's girlhoods and adulthoods. There was a question designed to elicit a sense of when they had felt most whole. I divided the messages that women received in childhood into "Open" messages such as those verbally communicated by a family member: for example, "You're dumb but beautiful," as well as disguised or implicit messages, which I called "Secret" messages, such as: "There are more opportunities for boys out there than for girls, so get married early." When I began to analyze the transcripts from my interviews I was shocked to discover that all of the women expressed to me an enhanced sense of well being, frequently available to them. They had true capacities for joy, as well as abilities to self replenish. All could reclaim, reintegrate and/or adapt positive states of being from their childhood into workable, pleasurable and often joyful adult states. It is these positive capacities that I have labeled THE ENCHANTED SELF.

These enhanced adult states of being were not repetitions of clearly identifiable ego states from childhood or adolescence, but were new integrations of elements of earlier positive conditions. They were a rebirth of a sense of well being in adult form.

Although my research has been limited to interviews with middle to upper class, white women, I have found that in my treatment room teaching and encouraging men how to access their ENCHANTED SELF has been beneficial and has worked well. In fact, THE ENCHANTED SELF technique has worked with all my clinical population, including children, when utilized in a timely fashion. All of us, whether men, women or children, need to know ourselves in authentic positive ways and to learn to recognize and encourage positive states of well-being. Because I have found THE ENCHANTED SELF paradigm shift so often useful in the treatment room in terms of helping clients access positive states of well-being and to see themselves in more positive ways, I have included several male treatment cases in this book. THE ENCHANTED SELF concept does not appear to be gender specific. Some men have indicated to me that they have a preference for viewing positive states of being as the enhanced self rather than THE ENCHANTED SELF. However, in general I have found both men and women responsive to THE ENCHANTED SELF and have therefore decided to use this term.

Why "THE ENCHANTED SELF"?

We have known that in any state of enchantment there is some degree of magic and the unknown: the Enchanted Forest looms dark and mysterious in fairy tales throughout the ages; princesses enchanted in fairy tales were touched by magic, whether for good or for evil. How could a kiss turn a toad into an enchanted prince? All of us who, as children, enjoyed fairy tales certainly believed a kiss could create a prince or awaken a princess who had been asleep for a hundred years. We could accept the idea of enchantment.

Many scientists of human behaviors recognize that we do not yet and perhaps never can fully understand human nature. I have become more and more convinced that we do not. For example, what interests me is that we do not fully understand why some people who have apparently fortunate lives experience little joy, while others, apparently less fortunate, experience great joy. Perhaps we have tried too hard to understand pathology in our science of psychology while we have not tried hard enough to recognize and understand what I call enhanced ego-states, or happiness.

When I first began to analyze data from the women I interviewed, I kept trying to understand how their enhanced adult lives evolved from the childhoods they talked about. I found that although there seemed to be some clear connections, many others were not clear at all. This mystery further influenced my choice of THE ENCHANTED SELF as a term to express these positive ego-states.

The capacities of these women to reclaim positive aspects of their childhood while discarding the dysfunction that was often also present was astounding to me. It seemed as if a magic wand had been tapped on the women's heads in their adult lives. I say this because many of the women were not naturally introspective. They did not seem to be aware that they had been able to reach into positive aspects of their childhoods to realize their adult dreams and to live vital lives much of the time. For example, Sally had grown up in a cold, dysfunctional household. She had promised herself that as an adult she would do things very differently from her parents. Her mother was a busy business woman who was cold and distant, while her father was extremely engaging to strangers but quiet and removed at home. In childhood, Sally was able to find her ENCHANTED SELF through her grandparents. As she got older, she would go back to their home after school, where she was nur-tured with milk and cookies and allowed to watch television in a happy, comfortable environment until she had to go to her home.

Sally talked lovingly of her visits with her grandparents. With plea-sure she mentioned being with them, and when she was left alone there she would "dance with a doorknob" as she rocked and rolled to a teenage show that she watched on TV every afternoon. She often felt let down when it was time to return to her own home.

In adulthood, Sally no longer "danced with a doorknob," but she found ways to honor her pledge to create a more meaningful and warm family life for her own children. Her children are adolescents now and feel free to bring their friends to spend time at her home. She doesn't push them away as she had been pushed away. Rather, she enjoys watching TV, playing games and talking and sharing with them as well as with their friends. On Saturday and Sunday mornings, she lies on the bed with them, laughing and gossiping. The capacity in her adult life to spend this joyful time with her teenagers overcomes the isolation she felt in childhood. Sally integrates the warmth and spunk of the times she spent at her grandparents into her adult ego. For Sally, there is no need to analyze this situation. She simply feels pleasure in having corrected the damaging childhood she'd experienced.

Of course, the recognition of pleasure does not appear only in adulthood; in fact, we feel positive mood states in early infancy before the capacity to retrieve memories clearly exists. An infant sucking eagerly at a breast or bottle, or lying contentedly in a parent's arms, or a toddler laughing with glee as someone plays hide-and-seek with her, is experiencing positive states of being that include positive body sensations as well as early forms of cognitive processing. However, because verbal memory is probably not involved, these states are not yet the full emergence of THE ENCHANTED SELF. In my theory, THE ENCHANTED SELF is clearly a capacity to retrieve, reintegrate and reorganize, in magical new formations, earlier memories and knowledge. What is important about early childhood in terms of THE ENCHANTED SELF is the first experiencing of positive states of being.

For example, the excitement a child feels dressed in a costume, going up to a neighbor's house asking for "Trick or Treat" on Halloween, can be very much an enhanced ego state. However, if he or she became frightened and there was no one waiting at the curb to provide safety, this positive ego state might have been interrupted in psychologically damaging ways. Thus, enhanced early states of being not only provide pleasure for the child but are critical stepping stones in the development of an integrated personality.

Other psychologists also talk about early enhanced ego-states and their importance. For example, in his book, *Getting the Love You Want*, Harville Hendrix[5] talks about "relaxed joyfulness, a state of full aliveness" that we all yearn to return to. In marital therapy he helps couples find ways to help each other get back to states of full aliveness. If the person can learn to relate to his or her spouse, without resorting to the negative patterns they grew up with, then they can respond to each other in warm, generous, loving ways. This will permit both parties to experience more of what Hendrix calls "relaxed joyfulness."

Again, whether we're talking about early elation as Ego psychologists, such as Margaret Mahler,[6] describe successful autonomous moments, or the relaxed joyfulness of the very young child before certain wounds take place, we are talking about early positive states of being.

It's hard to say exactly when these states become internalized as THE ENCHANTED SELF. More than likely, this will vary from person to person and is highly dependent on variations in cognitive development, particularly in memory. However, even for those people who have had less than adequate parenting, there are moments when children feel good about themselves: the baby is elated as she takes her first steps, the toddler feels joy as she rides a tricycle 20 feet down the driveway. Children are excited the day they first earn their own money for small jobs, the day they save a kitten from a tree and return it to its grateful owner, the day they successfully down the bully on the playground.

Of course, as one acquires more language, one may hold onto these positive moments and remember them. Also, the capacity for a sense of well-being has been experienced and, can be tapped into again in adulthood. This capacity to draw from positive memories seems especially magical when we realize that most people's moments of pure childhood joy have been surrounded by dysfunction.

Notions of the Child Within, the Real Self, True Self, Inner Child, Deepest Self and Inner Core have all been used interchangeably for many years. As Charles L. Whitfield states in his book, *Healing the Child Within*,[7] "the Child Within refers to that part of each of us that is ultimately alive, energetic, creative and fulfilled: it is our Real Self – who we really are."

THE ENCHANTED SELF is not the "Inner Child." THE ENCHANTED SELF is, rather, a lifelong capacity for positive states of being. One's positive capacities wait to be reclaimed and re-integrated into current positive states.

When one is grieving or angry, one may be in touch with one's "Real Self;" however, THE ENCHANTED SELF might not be experienced at these times, because the person would have deep painful feelings such as grief or rage at the time. THE ENCHANTED SELF emerges during times of joy, confidence, courage, humor, inner peace, calm and many other positive moods.

At profound levels, incorporating core aspects of oneself with states of well-being would merge into what I call "THE SONG OF THE SOUL." On these occasions one would be singing one's SONG OF THE SOUL from the deepest recesses of one's "Inner Child," of "The Child Within," experiencing a sense of authenticity and wholeness.

As I interviewed women, I quickly became aware that many of us have a tendency to emphasize our present and early pathologies rather than highlighting our joyous feelings or our talents. This makes sense if we realize that emotionally we hold onto unfinished business rather than onto what has been successfully completed or experienced.

Some of the women I interviewed were not aware of their enhanced capacities for well-being until I pointed out to them certain enhanced capacities I had seen in their childhood, re-incorporated in positive fashions as adults. I began to realize as I listened, that THE ENCHANTED SELF was a capacity that could benefit from conscious learning and active practice.

For most of us, conscious learning and active practice are necessary both to achieve THE ENCHANTED SELF as well as to sing one's SONG OF THE SOUL. As Zelig Pliskin states in his book, *Begin Again Now*,[8] "... the awareness that much happiness is self-induced can lead to the determination to do everything possible to become a more positive thinker.... A champion positive thinker ... will live a life of joy."

For example, when Edith talked about her childhood, she at first remembered only its dysfunctional aspects: the fighting between her parents and their constant criticality. I suggested that we go back and look again at her childhood to identify times when in spite of the pain of family life, she felt excited about her own life and about herself. With that encouragement she could separate out positive memories of herself from dysfunctional family experiences and she remembered some wonderful times: delightful family picnics, fishing with her grandfather and shelling peas with her grandmother on the porch.

The magic was that the adult Edith could integrate the overly functional, meticulous child she once was into an enormously competent professional woman who gained positive self-esteem and gratification from her abilities. She even found the time to develop her talent for dancing. Thus Edith's ENCHANTED SELF in adulthood was really the successful integration of the compulsive traits created by negative childhood experiences, with old pleasures and new talents. How can we label such a variety of positive ego-states coming from such different reservoirs of human histories as anything but enhanted?

Even women who absorbed negative or restrictive messages from childhood about their roles in life achieved some capacity to reclaim positive ego-states. For example, Betty came from a home that taught girls to grow up and marry as quickly as possible. Education for girls was not valued. In spite of this, Betty's childhood was far from emotionally narrow. Her home was loving and safe. She knew her parents loved each other deeply. She had many exciting and brilliant relatives.

"It was so stimulating at my grandmother's house," Betty said. "I had an uncle who was a photographer, another uncle who was a brilliant surgeon, and an aunt who taught piano. In addition to these relatives, writers and doctors also visited. These very interesting people listened to my ideas. I was encouraged to use my mind and ask questions. I was respected."

Like many girls, Betty had been taught to please. Marrying at 17, of course she believed that marriage would be a fairy tale come true. When she and her husband did not get along in early marriage, she tried very hard to make herself a "good" person, trying to please him and others. Later, as she matured, she began to have more insight. For example, she realized suddenly that doing for everyone else and trying to make everyone happy was not making anyone happy, least of all herself. She then began taking better care of herself in many ways. She developed her creativity through art and spiritual development, which included taking class in a concept called *A Course in Miracles*, as well as other pursuits. Betty saw that as she developed herself, those around her also seemed happier.

A Course in Miracles taught Betty to provide herself with safer and firmer boundaries. For examples, she remembered this question from the course: "Would you let someone come into your home and throw paint on the walls?" This question has often helped center Betty as an older woman. She has gathered the courage to speak more directly to her husband and to those whom she must supervise. She has learned how to get her needs met, while respecting her sacred space. Betty has completed a high school equivalency diploma. She seeks learning from many sources now and, as a result, her personal wisdom is great. As she states, "My world goes way beyond this house and/or this marriage."

Although the messages she received in childhood led her to expect that she would lead a narrow life, this isn't how it turned out. Rather, she took the stimulating, respectful atmosphere she experienced at her grandparents', as well as the love she felt in her own home, into adulthood with her. "I wouldn't want to be young again," she says. "I wouldn't want to be any other age. I wouldn't want to go through the whole growth process again; I'd rather be where I am. I'm so much more aware and conscious. I'm not caught up in what is going on out there. I have a life that's very much my own."

Turning my gaze into the treatment room

The women I interviewed caused me to look at my clients in new ways. As Proust[9] states, "The real voyage of discovery consists not in seeking new landscapes, but in having new eyes." I discovered many aspects of enchantment in my clients as I began to look anew at them. I began to recognize, within my treatment room, extraordinary human beings. Yes, they often had difficult life situations, dysfunctional backgrounds, poorly functioning and damaging marriages, problem children and other disappointments, but they were still able to achieve many moments that worked well for them. Here were people who felt passion and excitement about many aspects of their lives.

What I saw led me to agree with those innovative professionals who have challenged the "disease" model, i.e.: the old way of looking at our clients or patients as primarily having problems, difficulties, dysfunctions, personality disorders or sickness. Classification numbers seem to be attached to them, labeling them as if they were items of clothing hanging from a department store rack. I began to perceive my clients differently, as if through a new lens – as people who have talents, who are survivors. They came equipped with a multitude of talents, capacities, hobbies, knowledge and passions. In the histories of their lives they experienced many enhanced mental and/or physical states, even in far from ideal circumstances.

As children my clients may have had special, peaceful ways of feeling when they went fishing alone by a pond, or when they were watching a sunset. This contented ego state of the ten-year-old was one way they experienced their ENCHANTED SELVES. Retrieved in adulthood, this positive state of being can serve as one Positive Fingerprint of the Mind, available for adult reclaiming, reintegrating and adaptation into a form that would suit the emerging of THE ENCHANTED SELF in adulthood. I began to see that each person's Positive Fingerprints of the Mind and Positive Shadowprints are unique, as individual as one's fingerprints, utilizing different positive capacities within them.

The women I interviewed made me aware of how we can forget what it felt like to be experiencing one's ENCHANTED SELF. The way we were raised in our particular family may get in the way of recognition. This is particularly true if one's family has dismissed something a child once loved to do, as being unimportant. For example, one might have enjoyed daydreaming while sitting in a swing. An irritated mother, calling from the back door, might have felt such an activity to be an unwise use of time. Someone else may have longed to be an artist or writer, but her family discouraged such "impractical" dreams. Another may have felt whole and pure while organizing a chaotic home life. Although not an ideal circumstance, the competencies one experienced and the sense of power may well have been another Positive Fingerprint of the Mind.

I began to realize that we, as therapists, need to understand, as well as help our clients to understand, that many of our earlier integrated moments, hours, days, weeks, our "optimizing opportunities" may have long been forgotten and discarded, the discarding aided by family as well as societal values, opinions and options. Each of my clients may not have had the chance, in terms of personal growth and education, to recognize or validate his or her Positive Fingerprints. But, still, enhanced times have happened. Inside of each client is an ENCHANTED SELF.

My new assignment as a therapist

Now it has become my job and my privilege to help sift through the layers of dysfunction and disturbance to help my clients to recognize, name, validate and integrate, as parts of themselves, these wellness capacities. This becomes the exciting, sleuthing job of the therapist. I search for and acknowledge what is already working for the client, or what did work in the past. Finding the good news about my client helps to re-balance the whole person.

This certainly doesn't mean that much of my work isn't the "traditional" work of the therapist. People still legitimately come in with problems and obvious dysfunctional personality patterns, anxieties, developmental issues and, at times, more severe pathologies, such as dissociative disorders or psychotic processing. All must be attended to. Of course, in helping my clients heal, I still assist clients in working through, interpreting and gaining insight from their own histories. Much of the work is painful. But, more than anything, I'm looking for those grains of sand that can turn into pearls, with a little guidance!

Chapter Two

The Therapist's ENCHANTED SELF Emerges

S INCE learning to view my clients as enchanted human beings, I've begun my own voyage of self-discovery and growth, leading me to become a much more joyful person as well as a healed one. I believe that most therapists' mental health improves as they listen to THE ENCHANTED SELF within their clients. It's a way for them to start on a more sacred journey in their own development while providing better therapy for their clients.

As we start on this adventure together, I want to share with you three important threads in my own development. The first is the dysfunction that I experienced in my family of origin in terms of my development as a woman. This early and continued contamination was certainly one of the major thrusts in my determination to become a therapist. I have written this section from my girlhood vantage point so that my early impressions and reactions can come alive, untainted by maturity and/or professionalism.

The second thread is my experience as a psychotherapy patient. This is important because it was through these experiences that I became profoundly aware of some of what can be missing in standard practice. Although this section is in many ways unique to me, similar experiences have been expressed by other women. After taking you through these two threads in my life, I hope you will begin to understand how I came to the curve in the road that led me to interview women outside my private practice.

The third thread I want to share is the way in which I have changed as a therapist and as a person since I began to recognize THE ENCHANTED SELF capacity circling back and forth among my interviewees, my clients and myself.

As I share aspects of myself with you, you'll have an opportunity, utilizing the exercises that follow each chapter, to share in the process of self-discovery.

My family of origin[10], written from early girlhood impressions

In my family of origin, families were unsafe havens, perhaps less so for a girl, but definitely for a woman; no question about it. You had to learn to fly and get out by the time you were between fourteen and twenty, at the latest. When I was a child, the only people who seemed to have any safe haven within family life were men. Men were catered to. They were served first, they always got the biggest portions of meat or chicken; they had their underwear folded for them and their socks sorted and their teacups carried to and from the kitchen table. Best of all, they could leave every day; they got to go somewhere. They got out.

I thought the women who stayed at home were caught in small, narrow lives that seemed fruitless and powerless. Until she went to college when I was six, my mother was one of them. Both my parents were ecstatic when my mother left our home to start her college education. She was leaving stagnant waters. It was clear to me that there was nothing for her in the house. Although a wonderful cook, she didn't really enjoy other household tasks. She had married at nineteen, leaving behind hundreds of miles away, all of her family. I knew this made her sad and lonely. She didn't like to be alone all day and she had no desire to make handicrafts, can fruit or plant anything.

There was nothing for a woman in the house – nothing. It was bleak, it was lonely, it was a slow death. It seemed better to walk out in front of a car and be killed immediately than to stay at home.

I assumed that my mother, my father and I knew it was the same at my Aunt Stella's house. We knew from our visits to her in California every summer. She cleaned the kitchen well and she served bagels and lox to my Uncle Dan every Sunday morning. It seemed Aunt Stella was mistreated. Uncle Dan yelled at her. I didn't understand why. She was so kind to me.

Aunt Stella got a kidney disease. She had operations. She had medicine that didn't work. Then she died, a slow, painful death and everyone knew − certainly my mother and father and I − that her life had been thwarted.

My Cousin Gert also lived a dismal life on a small farm with Joe who earned very little money. Gert had to get up early and help him milk cows and collect eggs. He always yelled at her. Then he had an affair. Gert didn't get very much from staying at home. Then Joe left her. She had to sell the farm and go live in a small, dark apartment near her brother. She seemed unhappy.

My Aunt Anna seemed to have something good going for her − at least Aunt Anna and her husband had money. Nobody was quite sure why her life seemed better than the others', though money probably was the reason. Aunt Anna was bright and articulate. But Aunt Anna had a temper. She got upset and angry and cried a lot. She picked fights with my mother and made my mother cry, too. My mother, father and I agreed that she wasn't a very happy person. She hadn't accomplished anything, had she? Yet I really loved Aunt Anna. I was confused about her. Why wasn't she happier? Would she yell at me? I hoped not.

We didn't see my father's mother as having failed. An immigrant woman who'd never really learned to speak English, she had a life just a few blocks wide. Still, she had brought up a wonderful son who was my father, hadn't she? Yet, she was locked into undesirable choices. If only she had learned English or if she hadn't been so frightened of a new culture, she could have done things differently, we believed. She should have learned to speak fluent English. Yiddish was passé! My father spoke Yiddish to his mother because he loved her − but never to me − because he loved me and I was an American! My mother, my father and I all knew that.

Look at my mother's mother. A talented young architect, grandpa's business had failed in the Depression. They often had to borrow money from my Uncle Irving and when they inherited money they spent it within a year or two, just to live. But my grandmother had been a beautiful, talented young woman who played the piano and had gone to a music conservatory to study for a year after high school. Then she got married and stopped playing the piano! It was sad, she didn't have to stop. Here she was, we thought, a nobody, living in Baltimore, Maryland, in a small, dinky apartment, when she had once been a beautiful, talented, young pianist. Why didn't grandma continue to play piano? I didn't understand.

I felt bad that she lived such a narrow life. And yet my love for her knew no bounds. She sang "God Bless America" to me as we sat on the porch in the warm spring evening. And she always let me "make up" music on her piano. I learned to create tunes that sounded harmonic and oriental at the same time, by using the black keys. I was her star, her precious one. "Tell me another story, Grandma, about living in Chelsea and being the oldest of nine children and when the seamstress came to make dresses, and the two maids heating the irons on the fire. Tell me about the reed organ at the end of the long, open playroom on the third floor! Tell me again how the kitchen roof could roll back and expose the sky on the Jewish holiday of Sukot so that all the children could hang vegetables and fruits from crossbeams and sit on Great Grandpa's lap! Tell me about the trolley-car with the straw seats in the summer that took you for the piano lessons you loved! And tell how Grandpa fell in love with you when you dropped your pin in the snow after a party!"

Grandpa was so good to me. He introduced me to tweety, a little sparrow that came and sat on the porch rail with us every day. He stayed up all night with me, sitting on a straight chair next to me, when I had the whooping cough. I knew they loved each other. I loved both of them so much.

Grandma, you gave me everlasting love. Why did you seem thwarted? I was angry, not at you, but at the circumstances of your life.

Then there was Aunt June. She was a star in the family. My father said she was a "mensch,"[11] just like my Great Grandmother. My mother's grandmother had been a "mensch." These were women with real heart and soul, who were kind and gracious and knew how to make you feel welcome. There was something about them that was inspiring to me when I heard my father talk about them. They had achieved something "beyond" – beyond family fighting and despair. He valued this "beyond" and he encouraged this quality in my mother. He pleaded with her to develop herself and he criticized her when she didn't seem to have enough "mensch-ness" for him. I don't know how he thought that putting her down would help her to go out and become an American-style "mensch."[11] Somehow, even if Mother didn't, I would ... that was clear. My father and I were together on that one.

We seemed to agree that the women who had made the most pf herself other than the two "menchen" was Cousin Toby. Cousin Toby became a gem appraiser and made a lot of money buying and selling diamonds. First it was ten thousand then thirty thousand then one-hundred thousand dollars! Now she was somebody. She had accomplished something in her life. We envied and adored her.

Obviously, a woman had to find a way to become her own person outside of the family because there was no way within the family. Outside, she would not be consumed, eaten up by disease or despair.

It now seems strange and puzzling, almost shocking, to look back and realize that my parents and I were the victims of a shared deception. I'm sure that what we saw – women, trapped in unsafe places, was what we now call family (and social) dysfunction.

Uncle Dan, Aunt Stella's husband, was difficult by any standards, and Gert and Joe must have had profound problems in their marriage. Aunt Anna had wanted to be a teacher and was not able to train. She married instead. Perhaps her keen intelligence and longings to help others had been thwarted, resulting in moods and angry outbursts. My mother's mother and father argued all the time, wearing Grandmother down. She could have played the piano; many women stayed involved in music in that generation, teaching or simply playing for pleasure. She stopped playing because of emotional and marital difficulties.

All of these women lived lives of pain, not because they chose to, or because they happened to be at home, but because of the intense personal and familial dysfunction as well as that caused by society's restraints on women. This was sad for my mother, my father and for me. They didn't know always how to be kind to each other, in the early years, or how to always create a sense of harmony within our home. They were loving and devoted to me. Even though I experienced being loved, it was difficult for me to start adult life with the emotional tools and attitudes necessary to negotiate early marriage. It's amazing that my husband, Russell and I have found real pleasure over the years. Of course, psychotherapy helped.

For Russell and me, individual and couple therapy were both essential to our marriage. Individual therapy helped each of us realize that the demands we were making on each other were often unrealistic, while couple's therapy helped us to see how our personality styles interacted. Many factors sustained us along with the encouragement and support of our therapies:

1) We deeply believed that we loved each other and saw ourselves as sharing similar values, both professionally and ethically. (Russ is also a psychologist.)
2) We believed in the institution of marriage as significant and deeply important to both of us.
3) We were both committed to spending our time as mental health providers and we felt a commitment in our personal lives to grow as individuals, as we wished to see our clients grow. Over the years, we have never violated each other in major ways, and we stand united as best friends. In his role as a marriage therapist, Russell, often talks about the "glue" between people. There is a lot of glue between us.

Reader's exercise

Relax and let your mind drift backward in time. Give yourself permission to drift back to a younger age. Let your intuition be your guide in choosing an appropriate age. Once you have chosen, imagine yourself in a room in a childhood home. See the furniture, the colors of the room. Can you smell anything, any aromas of food cooking or other odors? Can you hear any noises or people talking? Is there a television on? What show might be on? Can you look out the window from where you're sitting? What do you see?

Take a couple of minutes to re-experience this childhood scene.

On a piece of paper, jot down all the positive thoughts and feelings you associate with this reflection. Then make a list of all the talents and positive capacities you had as a child at that age, whether they were recognized by anyone else in the world or just secretly and intuitively recognized by you.

Chapter Three

Myself as a Client

L IKE so many others who become therapists, I left my dysfunctional childhood behind in search of correction. My deep desire to heal my wounds made me eager to become a healer. As a young woman in my twenties, I found myself wanting to become a teacher and actually taught first and second grades, but quickly moved on, yearning for a more intimate entrance into another world. I longed to become a repairer of the heart, a piano tuner of the mind. And, of course, my own therapy, or should I say therapies, accompanied these explorations.

First of these, at the end of my freshman year in college, was therapy with a psychiatrist who had been a friend of my father's, who saw me as a favor to my dad. He was a handsome and wise man. I told him only what I felt comfortable talking about. I kept secret many feelings, including sexual attraction for him and my intense inferiority feelings. He helped me to clarify my thoughts about transferring to the college of my choice. Then the therapy terminated. I'd never shared my inner life with him at all – I wouldn't have dared, for reasons I can't fully put into words.

Then there was a psychiatrist at Barnard College who came in one morning a week. He took voluminous notes. Did he have a voice? Yes, he did. He called me Miss Becker. The two times he did speak to me beyond utterances of "uh huh" and "yes," he spoke wisely and profoundly. On each occasion, I made drastic changes in my life. I felt no emotional connection with him, but somehow he was able to nurture me and provide some critical guidance. Yet I still secretly saw myself as a weed.

Next was a psychiatrist I sought out in early marriage, when I was a graduate student in Boston. He called me Mrs. Holstein. He, too, said little, but he was warmer and took fewer notes! He was truly liberating in that he seemed to think I was intelligent. He encouraged my doctoral training as well as other interests and hobbies. I actually flowered while seeing him. I still felt separate and less than he, but no longer a weed. I was really a flower!

Later, after I became a psychologist, there were two significant therapists in my life. The first one provided me with individual as well as couple's and group therapy experiences. He was warm and frank and capable of making a good connection with me. I grew a great deal while I worked with him, obtaining my post-doctorate psychology training and becoming licensed.

The licensing exam was a nightmare for me. I easily passed the written exam, but failed the oral. This experience necessitated further intensive therapy. It was during this time, with my therapist's guidance, that I became aware of and began to work through my own deeply embedded anxieties around achievement, as a woman. My feelings of panic about success and professional status were tied into very old memories of my family and the ways in which women lived and were perceived. Emotionally released, at least to the extent that I understood that my parents did not really want me to fail professionally, I was finally able to pass the oral exam.

Ultimately, it was this terrifying exam process that began my interest in women's issues. Certainly I'd experienced more anxiety in the oral exam than most of my male counterparts had. When asked a question, I was only too eager to be ingratiating and to listen very carefully to the nuances of the question so that I could match my response to what I thought the examiner wanted to hear. I thought I was being very genuine, concerned and judicious. Later, in my feminist readings, I discovered that my gender learning had worked against me. In the oral exam, I appeared uncertain and "self-deprecating," according to feedback from a male examiner. When I finally passed the oral part of the licensing exam, I had fought through at the deepest psychological levels my anxiety over becoming a professional woman. I had also fought a gender battle which left me finally understanding the experience of violation that so many women feel as they attempt to plan out how they're going to expend their energies in life – in the service of what goals and identities.

I've never forgotten the pain I suffered knowing that I was so misjudged by my colleagues. Later, when I began to interview women outside of my practice, one thread I carried within me was the sense of violation I had felt. This was a violation that went beyond already disheartening family messages and further damaged the very fabric of my adult female experience.

My final therapist was an older, semi-retired man who offered me support in a nonjudgmental, gentle fashion. Psychodynamically oriented, he seemed to use a mildly hypnotic technique that permitted me, for the first time therapeutically, to share all that had remained censored, all that I felt still poisoned me. As words emerged from my mouth, none of the poison-balls turned into anything more than dust puffs. I felt miraculously cleansed of mental debris, and emerged sure that I was a beautiful flower.

Looking back at my various therapies, I can identify the first three as psychoanalytic approaches encouraging growth. Indeed, I did grow in each. However, in the first two, I experienced violation. The psychiatrists remained distant and remote. Their stances further intensified secret feelings that I was already contaminated. The third psychiatrist was more comfortable with an informal approach. He shared bits and pieces of his own life, his marriage and his children. I felt respected by him in a mildly connected way. He also encouraged my talents, rather than identifying them as defense mechanisms. My perfectionistic and compulsive tendencies were encouraged by him inasmuch as they provided the persistence to complete my doctoral dissertation. He gave me hope that I would continue to evolve in positive ways as I grew older.

The psychologist who saw me in individual, couple's and group therapy also had an informal style that helped me to feel a part of the real world. His approach was eclectic, but also psychodynamically oriented. He called me by my first name and his sincere interest in my development was clear. He supported talents and old patterns of wellness, rather than discouraging them. However, I felt he made clear that behind my strengths lurked dysfunction at the family as well as at the personal level. In other words, even though he encouraged me, I perceived an assumption that I was made up of less than ideal attributes. Still, I made an effort to be totally honest with this clinician, having realized how much of my material I'd censored in the past. However, his style, which was to dialogue, did not permit me a full flow. It was clear to my unconscious, as well as my conscious, that he knew more than I did. Thus, at some deep level, I was left feeling unsure of my own capacities. Also, his parental style, although supportive and often right on target, left me feeling as if I were a flower with a petal out of shape, which I was trying to hide.

My last therapist let the flow go on long enough for me to develop internalized integrity. I felt respected as a professional and as a woman. He encouraged talents without looking for negative qualities. I was able to leave feeling a great deal of personal strength. What I still did not feel was a sense of safety and purpose within my world, which included not only my husband and children but my professional life as a therapist and as a woman in our society. But I felt that I was no longer the problem. I was a lovely flower. It was the garden itself that was lacking. There wasn't enough sunlight; I couldn't see clearly enough how I fit in. I was not being fully nurtured; at times I felt cold and barren and began to sense that I had internalized the barrenness. At forty-five, I experienced a hole within myself. However, at the conscious and unconscious levels, I was still moving toward further healing. This self healing led to discovery of THE ENCHANTED SELF.

Reader's exercise

Again, scan your childhood for the choice of an age level you wish to focus on. I would advise listening to your intuition in this choice. Once you have an age in mind, dwell a few moments on yourself at that age. See yourself going to school, playing with friends, being at home. Perhaps you can imagine yourself in Sunday School or at summer camp or with your grandparents. Again, let your instincts lead you to a variety of activities and scenes which were significant, yet, at the same time, commonplace for you. Now think about the following questions – you may want to write down your answers so that you can refer to them later:

1. What were your beliefs when you were a child around the age you've just recalled? Whom were you supposed to be when you grew up?

2. What were your parents' and/or your family's expectations for you?

3. What do you think your parents' or your family's beliefs were as to whom you were supposed to become when you grew up?

4. What neighborhood and/or cultural beliefs about one's role as an adult female or male were you intuitively or explicitly aware of as a child at around the age pictured?

Chapter Four

Discovering THE ENCHANTED SELF

M Y desire to interview women outside of my private practice was a spontaneous shot in the dark, a leap from my unconscious. I knew I wanted to get to know women in a way that took me beyond the treatment room. I knew I wanted to feel relaxed and able to share in an unguarded way impossible in the therapist mode. I knew I wanted change and growth in my own life. I was not seeking a new career; I knew I wanted to remain a therapist, that I was a piano tuner of the mind. Beyond that, I didn't know what I wanted.

When I looked back, at age forty-five, at how my therapies ended, I think I felt a sense of betrayal. I felt a sense of isolation in my world. I felt as if I were climbing uphill backwards, unable to see clearly. I was always strained and tired. There seemed to be a hole inside me. My life lacked a feeling of safety and of correct fit. I didn't have the clean, sure feeling of a cat crossing a patio or a machine that moves flawlessly as if filled with liquid mercury. My life still felt rough and edgy as I moved through it.

What was it that I didn't yet understand about myself? My life? My profession? My role as a woman? Something wasn't reaching me, seemed to be withheld from me; some information was still not being processed. When I look back now, the questions I asked the women I interviewed certainly reflected my quest to find out what was missing in my own life.

The questions I asked

I wanted to know more about the roles assigned to girls and what messages they received about what their roles in adulthood would be like. I wanted to know how these messages affected them by the time they were adults. When had they been happiest as children? As adults? What family of origin patterns of behavior had they brought to significant relationships, such as marriage? Had they lived out any special dreams? When did they feel most whole? What would they do differently if they could live it over again? What would they attempt to teach their children and grandchildren? My husband was extremely helpful as I developed the questions I wanted to ask the women, and he gave me encouragement to go out and interview them. I think he, too, sensed my hunger and my need.

Beginning to interview the women was a breakthrough for me. Going to their offices or meeting with them over lunch or dinner, or going to their homes, taping their responses, analyzing them – it was all so refreshing. When I sat with them I felt eager yet relaxed, and when I looked at the responses, I felt real excitement as I saw certain patterns emerging. The wonder I experienced when I began to see the joy and self-fulfillment that so many of these women had achieved! I found myself uplifted and resonating to their joy. I was finally really turned on.

Beginning to reclaim my ENCHANTED SELF

My ENCHANTED SELF was beginning to emerge, unpeeling as an onion is unpeeled, layer by layer. This is important because I think so many of us shy away from our innermost positive feelings perhaps as much as we do from the dark shadows around us. The search for THE ENCHANTED SELF is intimate and revealing and it's scary – and maybe people really won't understand or appreciate it. Maybe we have to fight through shame or humiliation before we find it. Maybe we won't understand or give credit to our own ENCHANTED SELVES when we do! That would be the most violating thing of all, if I were to find my own ENCHANTED SELF and then discard it. If I can't have it anymore, because I've thrown it out.

One of my first self-discoveries was recognizing my lost capacity for engaging with people without being paid. As I interviewed the women I realized how much fun I was having, how I felt on equal footing and yet privileged to be hearing their stories, how "female" I felt and how connected. I loved this wonderful opportunity to have time with women that was not social time and yet not work time, either. I began to realize how hungry I had been for this kind of "at ease time" with women. My childhood had pushed me away from such time with women. After all, I had to get out, to get going, to become competent and, often, competitive, not connected.

The second layer was feeling profoundly more connected to women, all women, than I had ever felt before. I found myself suddenly able to ally myself with and have compassion for many women, an ability which had eluded me prior to these interviews. Family members, friends, my mother, all took on a softer hue.

As therapists, we can certainly wonder why this hadn't happened as a result of my training and my time in therapy. After all, I had been exposed to hundreds and hundreds of intimate stories over fifteen years. My hunch is that while in the treatment room, I, like any paid healing professional, saw myself, to some extent, as being in the authority position. This may have reinforced some natural biases that I carried with me from my childhood. I think I continued to withhold some deep level of empathy, still seeing myself as being apart. When interviewing the women, however, I was automatically their equal, and that placed me differently. Having the privilege of listening to the 18 women, began to listen to other women's voices with less bias and value judgments. For example, I had always valued certain capacities, such as pragmatic decision-making and the capacity to carry through once a decision had been made. This is a capacity which can be restricted for women. After this glimpse into the girlhood dreams and shattered hopes of many of the women interviewed – the compromises made with life and the painful, yet successful ways of salvaging one's soul after many lost

29

opportunities – I was able to cross a barrier and join them at some level of womanhood – removing my own iron bars, my negativity and judgments.

The third unwrapping came when I needed major surgery, an emergency hysterectomy. I found myself able to permit women to nurture me through this emergency in a way that I don't think I was able to do before I began this project. I no longer felt I needed to rely on the authority of the male. I yearned for the caretaking, nurturing capacities that many women offer so much more freely than do most men. My surgeon was a woman and I insisted on private-duty female nurses for a while. I allowed them to cradle me, soothe me, massage me and nurse me.

The next layer that was reached was my capacity to run my practice differently, as I recovered from the hysterectomy. I was able to relinquish some of my controls and to soften professional/client boundaries as appropriate. I gave them the best that I could while still being totally honest. While I was in a recovery state I saw clients in my living room or provided telephone sessions. I put my feet up; I accepted gifts and food from clients. I let them nourish me and take care of me for a while.

During this time, my clients and I shared our competencies. They even paced their subject matter to my recovery level. Usually this was done without explanation. I accepted their pacing as one of the beautiful gifts they were able to offer me. As I grew stronger, their problems reemerged in ways I was able to cope with. They reparented me into recovery as I had attempted to reparent them before my sudden surgery. From women clients came gifts and cards and the presentation of beautiful sweets. All were accepted with joy and from the heart. I made no attempt to interpret them, which I thought would have been demeaning because these tokens came out of mutual caring. To have tried to interpret this material as transferential would have been a diminishment of our humanity. If need be, I could always use this material again, anyway. And if some transferential material never reemerged, what a small price to pay, to give so many of my clients an opportunity to show their competencies and caring. Most were able, with grace, to rely on their own capacities while still being aware that they were staying in treatment not to have tea with me but to further heal and grow. In helping me heal, I believe they felt empowered.

My ENCHANTED SELF emerges and grows

The next achievement of my ENCHANTED SELF journey was permitting myself to retrieve some of my own lost ambition and interests. Instead of using logic, I went to a deeper level, relying on an inner sense of what I needed. I permitted myself to sense what felt right to reach back for, to pursue and to honor.

I went to a Shiatsu workshop to learn hands-on healing and touching skills. Feeling their breathing and having skin contact with others without in any way violating them was replenishing and bonding. Touching was a revelation after sitting across the room from people for so many years. In our society there is so little physical contact among friends and even within some families. This was a new and healing experience that I was happy to bring home to share with my husband, friends and family.

I also went on a five day religious retreat where I was finally able to pursue questions I had about my religion (Judaism) as well as to experience spiritual aspects of Jewish worship for the first time since I was sixteen.

This experience led to yet another layer, which was my birthday treat with my cousin, Joann. (Our birthdays are two weeks apart). I wanted to know how Judaism could feel as one lived it. I was Jewish, but no one had ever taught me the passion or the soul, of being Jewish. Joann offered me a chance to go with her for a weekend to live with an orthodox Jewish family in another community. I came away moved, uplifted and convinced that feminism has ancient roots.

The orthodox family had no television and lived, compared to me, very private lives based on Torah teachings where daily life is sanctified through prayer. Rachel and her husband treated each other with respect. Each gave the other center stage on many occasions. No public criticisms or put-downs took place. Their eight children were also treated (and treated others) with respect and caring. Older children helped younger ones. At times there was normal anger and frustration among siblings, but they didn't call each other names or speak harshly. When conflicts developed, the older children often intervened with healthy techniques such as distracting their younger siblings. At one point fourteen children played earnestly at one end of the living room while four adult women conversed actively at the other end of the room. We were actually able to hear one another! Something positive was going on, something I rarely saw. There was something there, in that culture, that was worth retrieving and knowing more about.

I realized that I had not permitted myself to consider seeing a female therapist, probably because I projected my negative feelings about being female onto women therapists. By never having worked with a woman on my inner life, I had denied myself a role model and validation as a woman. This is a common dilemma for women in our society: our learned self-hatred keeps us away from deep connections with other women, although this is changing, in part because of women's groups of all kinds that began with consciousness-raising groups.

My own perceptions about women were rarely challenged. I lived silently with my distortions and, given the nature of my therapies, my family's message that women were powerless, inadequate and lived in an unsafe world, could not emerge in a way that would have permitted me to change. I needed knowledge about women and their power, and I needed at least some of that knowledge to come from other women.

The larger world provided me with little knowledge about women's development of how knowledge was transmitted from wise woman to ingenue. Little "wise-woman" knowledge had been transmitted to me. As Lerner so beautifully states in her book,[12] each generation of women has had to rediscover themselves. Precious time has been lost because we don't share a matrix of knowledge about our world, as men do. All the history that we are taught about the world, our country, our society, is based on men's perceptions and their choice of what should be transmitted as truth. My preoccupation with achievement and professional growth left me disconnected from the wisdom of women.

My ENCHANTED SELF continues to grow

Even with all the new experiences I allowed myself since my therapies had terminated, a unifying thread for my ENCHANTED SELF had yet to appear. At a critical moment, a female Torah teacher entered my life. Mrs. S. taught me to clarify my ENCHANTED SELF and to separate out "womanly" function from family dysfunction. Finally I had a role model, a woman who was in a deep reciprocal relationship with me. She was bright, caring, knowledgeable, sensitive and appropriate. She was able to help me lift the veil that lies over women. Through Judaic concepts of God and Godliness, as well as in the Torah stories of Jewish women, I found my true identity.

About the same time that I began to work with her, I read *The Feminist Face of God*[13] by Sherry Ruth Anderson and Patricia Hopkins. These authors stirred my imagination by expanding the notion of God to include a feminine side. Through powerful images, including dream material, the authors conveyed the notion that God, as well as the world, yearns and waits for women to utilize their feminine attributes of wisdom, compassion, understanding and sensitivity in ways that can save the world.

Mrs. S. was able to help me further understand that, as far back as the earliest Jewish recorded history, women were viewed in the Torah as having wisdom and judgment capacities far beyond men's. When God wanted Moses to accept the Torah, He asked Moses to present the Torah to the women and ask them to accept it. We believe God's reasoning was that if the women accepted the Torah they would have the wisdom and the gentleness to guide and motivate those around them to live by the Torah's principles.

Women were considered to be so deeply in touch with God's holy presence that they did not need to pray many times a day upon command, as did the men. Instead, they were required only to say certain specific prayers. It was understood that women's natures were deeply spiritual and that they did not need the formal controls that men needed. For example, God's holy presence is with a woman when she lights the Sabbath candles. She can then pray directly from her heart about what is important to her.

Women in Judaism have been prophetic. Deborah, for one, was a prophet as well as extremely wise. All the learned men came to her for advice and wisdom and she became the judge for the entire nation. There were many other clever Biblical women and unusually talented young girls. For example, Miriam was only a child at the time she figured out a plan to keep husbands interested in their wives, even while they were burdened by slavery in Egypt, so that children would continue to be born. Miriam had the women fix themselves up and take mirrors to where the men were working in the fields. The women could hold their mirrors at an angle so that the husbands could see their wives' reflections even as they toiled. That way, they became aroused and interested again.

As I worked with Mrs. Shaingarten week by week, she told me about Jewish women, their wisdom and courage and their capacities for connecting to the divine presence at the deepest spiritual levels. Her words gave me a sense of self-confirmation and self-renewal. These women were role models with all the beautiful and profoundly varied traits which, as a child, I knew intuitively should be desirable and "normal" for women. But these traits were not valued in my dysfunctional family.

My perceptions of women were quickly and profoundly changing. The women I'd interviewed, my clients, my own search for a reemergence of buried parts of myself had all led to changed perceptions about psychotherapeutic treatment as well as about what constituted enhanced adult life, at least for me. I had many moments of deep insight. I was traveling on my own personal enchanted voyage and it was a marvelous journey.

Yet another moment of insight was generated by my cousin Joann's story about her childhood, "A Balabusta Coming Full Circle."[14] As I read Joann's story, I realized that she was a woman who had identified with her mother and also respected her parents' life together and what they had been able to offer her. I had grown up loved but feeling disempowered. Joann saw herself as coming from a long line of competent, fiery, strong women.

"I am indeed blessed because on both my mother's and father's side, I come from a prestigious line of balabustas[15] ... My grandmothers were probably, if there is such a thing, balabusta mavens — the royalty of balabustaism," Joann had written.

Unlike Joann, I was unable to identify with the women in my family because I saw them as weak, powerless and without firm identities. Also, I'd felt that when I was in touch with my more competent qualities, which included being ambitious, in charge and feeling powerful, somehow I felt "masculine." In other words, I had absorbed a "Silent Message" in childhood that to be an achiever and a doer and by being truly involved and excited in what one did (especially in the outside world), was "masculine." Until I was able to really reframe and broaden the concept of being female, helped by the ancient Judaic concepts of a woman incorporating all sorts of talents and capacities as well as nurturing abilities and spirituality, only then was I able to get back to myself and name myself properly.

In not naming myself properly, I could not validate what was most enchanted about myself because it put me in conflict. We all know the dangers and pain of feeling conflicted and how we run from it. My latest enchanted insight has been my recognition of my ENCHANTED SELF as an ENCHANTED WOMAN – and how good that feels! I realize that I'm beginning to sing at least one verse of my SONG OF THE SOUL.

Reader's exercise

This time you're going to scan your childhood, rather than focusing on a particular age, while you answer the following questions. Again, you may want to make some notes or keep a list so that you can use your self-knowledge later.

1. What were some of the Open Messages you were given about what you should become when you grew up, i.e., messages clearly stated by a family member or by society at large?

2. What were some of the Silent or Secret Messages you absorbed in childhood about what you should become when you grew up, i.e., unstated messages but still intuitively understood by you?

3. Do you have any intuitive hunches as to which messages, if any, may have gotten in your way as you developed? If you have realized that a particular message interfered with your development, please jot it down so that in a later exercise we can start to reframe your talents and positive capacities.

Chapter Five

Helping THE ENCHANTED SELF Emerge in the Treatment Room

As time went on, I began to see clues related to THE ENCHANTED SELF for other therapists, and for their clients. I was beginning to understand that ordinary people, both women and men, can lead private, yet extraordinary, lives. I was becoming convinced that therapists do not fully understand or learn to recognize the positive enhanced capacities of their clients. I began to understand that as therapists we do not look hard enough for the client's "golden nuggets" within her own past. Desires, hopes, talents, fleeting opportunities that may have been mislabeled in negative ways by the family of origin, or the client may have cast such lost "golden nuggets" into a place where if she returned there she might experience shame or humiliation or confusion. Good feelings may be lost in the bad. This had certainly happened to me.

I began intentionally to help my clients[16] to find their ENCHANTED SELVES. I found myself actively designing questions and opportunities to engage clients in sharing their enchanted sides. For example, I began to ask new clients to tell me about times in their lives when they had felt most whole, most productive, and most integrated.

Donna comes to mind: A bright married woman with two young daughters and an advanced degree, Donna was anxious and depressed. Having taken an executive job with a large corporation, she found herself caught in the jet stream of modern life, and her job was not nourishing her. She found her multiple roles in life fatiguing. Understandably, as she looked toward the future, she was not certain that she wanted to move toward a higher management position. To make matters worse, communication problems in her marriage were exacerbated when her children were born.

During her first session, Donna concluded her review of herself by saying, "I need help in sorting through my job goals and learning to interact better with my husband."

I asked her to tell me what some of the best times in her life had been, some of the times when she had felt most whole, when she felt most centered, perhaps experiencing some real joy. This question is central to Enchanted Self technique. Donna seemed a little surprised but then her eyes lit up, and she appeared actually peaceful. She reported two memories:

"I would say I was happiest growing up when I went to live with a family in England for a summer. I felt elated and super competent. I achieved and excelled. I also felt I had proven to myself that I could go beyond my own heritage. My parents had lived simply and had never traveled, and here I was, going off to England. And the experience itself was just as thrilling as winning the opportunity to go overseas! The other time when I felt really happy and whole was after the birth of my first child. Every day was a delight and made life really worth living. Just seeing her change and grow made it worth waking up."

I told Donna that she had just clearly illuminated two of the great capacities in life. One was the experience of validating one's own talents. The second was the wonderful opportunity of connection with another human being, which can fill a person with joy and hope in life. If we now worked toward recreating a stronger sense of those capacities in her present world – the threads of which extended back in time – she could regain a sense of well-being.

Another technique I developed was listening to what the client brought in to see if, within her narratives, she alluded to enchanted capacities about herself. Often a client would share significant information that could be overlooked if I were attempting to stay "on course," perhaps my own course, in the therapy. Mary illustrates this. She is a woman who suffered chronic anxiety and was uncertain of her identity. Her low self-esteem was fed by feelings of frustration and guilt about her learning-disabled daughter.

"I had a great time last week," Mary told me. "I went to Maine with a group of women I play cards with. I've been friendly with these women for years, but held back from them. I've been uneasy about sharing certain intimacies, particularly since we all know each other's children, and I have a daughter with learning problems. Usually, they plan to go on a five-day trip to coastal Maine when I'm busy working. But this year, in an effort to include me, they picked a different date. This put me in conflict. I was still hesitating when I mentioned it to my husband, and he said something like, 'Oh, you won't go, so what difference does it make?' Well, that did it. As soon as he said that, I knew I was going. That he should be so certain that I wouldn't go with my friends convinced me that I was ready to go!

Those five days were the best days in my adult life. We became the dearest of friends. We laughed and shared confidences and stayed up all night chatting just as I had with my best friends before I grew up! We supported each other and helped each other, but the best thing was being accepted for myself. I felt an authenticity as my own person rather than in my roles as wife, mother, or volunteer. I was really having a ball. I don't think our husbands understood the fun we had. I now have a new feeling about these women, a special sense that we connect and understand each other, that makes me feel more centered. I also have a new and special feeling about myself. As an aside, the interesting thing is that since I've been back, my daughter seems to have flowered. Perhaps it was coincidental, or perhaps I am more at ease with her."

I reinforced Mary's perception about how well she had related to her daughter. That might have been my only focus prior to the beginning of my ENCHANTED SELF journey as a therapist. But now I also encouraged her budding efforts to get back in touch with the fun-loving, connected, social, adaptable child and teenager who had been such a significant part of herself before marriage. Of course Mary could have made progress in her therapy even if we had just focused on her success in dealing more effectively with her daughter. And, although she recognized that being replenished by her friend-ships helped her to relate more effectively, that realization alone did not reinforce the positive aspects of herself experienced on the trip, which reclaimed earlier childhood strengths. My responses gave me an opportunity to help her reframe a lost part of herself. Reclaiming these strengths would begin a process for her of feeling whole and competent.

With Joe, a middle-aged client, I focused my long range goals dif-ferently than I might have in the past without the insights about ENCHANTED SELF therapy. Joe had a definite characterological difficulty: he lied to friends and family about certain events in his life. He lied to a point where he lived in fear that he would be exposed. We talked about this many times. I didn't mince words. I was very clear that his lying was damaging to his capacities for bonding with others. But I also pointed out that within his pathol-ogy there could be a silver lining: a talent for weaving tales. Having a great imagination is much valued in our culture. "Let's see what we can do with these traits over time," I told him.

As Joe's therapy continued, he stopped telling lies, reaching an important goal in the therapy. However, it wasn't until the end of therapy that his real pearl emerged. In fact, the day we terminated, he presented me with his solution around this capacity, and his plan for turning it into an enchanted thread within himself. He talked about becoming a weaver of tall-tales for his grandchildren. He couldn't wait until they sat at his knee to hear the fantastic fables he had to tell them.

Another client, Ann, spoke after several years of intense psy-chotherapy, a therapy that focused deeply on her dysfunctional extended family and the resultant problems she had experienced.

"I just read a book entitled *Flow*," Ann said. "I began to realize that I'm really in a happy state most of the time. I have many enjoyable hobbies and activities that engross me. I feel centered and have a sense of well being. However, I never really gave this major part of my life any credit because I knew I had difficulties and had failed in important relationships. I didn't view the happy moments with value. I think that may have been a mistake.

"Even though my family was incredibly dysfunctional, one thing I have to say for my nutty mother and aunt was that they exposed me to the enjoyment of hobbies and other interests. They were both always involved in projects, and they encouraged me to do likewise. It is amazing to me how people could have such incredible dysfunction and still offer me something that I enjoy every day of my life!"

Ann was looking back at her family and finding positive memories. She had a strong enough sense of self at this point in her therapy to be able to give credit where credit was due. Even though her family had damaged her in many ways, they had also shared their hobbies and talents with her, which she absorbed and incorporated into much of her daily life. Strong enough now to see the golden thread that connected herself to her mother and aunt, she could appreciate them for the many positive hours she already enjoys. Once Ann saw this positive thread in their joint history, corrective pattern of relating to her mother and aunt could slowly emerge.

In the chapters that follow I'd like to invite you to continue with me to learn how to discover and encourage THE ENCHANTED SELF in others as well as in yourself. Let my clients' voices, the women interviewed, and others who have come into my life, share with you the enhanced parts of themselves.

Reader's exercise

We are now on a journey of rediscovery: the search for your positive Fingerprints of the Mind. Again, I would suggest that you jot down your answers to the following questions so that you can utilize some of the positive memories later.

1. What were some golden moments in your childhood when you felt particularly happy? These moments can be from any age, from your earliest memories through early adulthood. When you find a golden memory, enjoy it. See yourself at that age and experiment with letting different senses reconnect to that happy time. Can you remember the way your body felt? Can you remember what activity you were engaged in? Were there any smells? What was the weather like? How did things look around you? What did your mood feel like? Take time to really enjoy this happy memory of yourself.

2. For those who would like to experience another positive memory retrieved from childhood, let me suggest that this time you

scan your past for a time when you were really having fun. When you find this time, take pleasure in it. What was going on around you at the time? What were you doing? What were you feeling inside? How did your body feel? What was the weather like? What was the scenery like? Were you with anyone? What were they like to be with? For those of you who may not have been able to come up with memories for questions 1 or 2, don't be discouraged. Sometimes positive memory retrieval has to develop with practice. Since your ENCHANTED SELF is often at least half hidden within the difficulties you had to put up with as a child, it can be elusive when you first try to find it. Stay with me.

Chapter Six

Helping Your Client Retrieve Positive Fingerprints

As I continued my journey of discovery, I realized there are several different ways to get in touch with positive states of being from the past. The most obvious pathway to retrieval is a person's memory bank of actual events. As I've already mentioned, we've all experienced positive states of being from earlier days even if they were surrounded by dysfunction. As I began my search for positive memories, many came back to me from my childhood and replenished me.

I remembered sitting in the back yard on the swing when I was eight, moving very slowly and comfortably as the sun beat down. I felt content. I remembered the scent of my skin after playing outside for hours and how much I enjoyed putting my hands and arms against my nose so I could smell the sweat. How I loved that mild, earthy aroma! I remember how good I felt sitting up in bed after a good sleep, with nowhere to go in the morning. I would gaze dreamily at the wallpaper. The flower pattern always looked as if it were saying the word "sale" over and over.

Other positive memories involved vigorous physical activity. I could ride my bicycle very fast down Buena Vista Road, with the wind blowing in my face. I took risks because I knew that I was a supercompetent bicyclist. I took risks roller-skating, too, again because I was so good at it. I could go really fast over the cracks. And even when I fell there was a feeling of delight. I was proud of the scabs on my knees and there was pleasure, too, in the recovery process. Kids love to anticipate the day when they can pick off the great big scab when it's ready to go. Waiting for the big scab was one of my secret childhood places of well being.

There were other secret states of well being, too. I could remember, for example, eating a really good steak one night, when my mother had cooked it just right. It was pinkish red and succulent. Boy, did she know how to cook beef! I got the big T-bone too! Oh, how I savoured the juices of that meat.

And then there were other moments. For example, memories of social well being that turned out to be momentously important to me. One was of the big day in the fourth grade when Angela agreed to be my best friend. She was my first best friend. The friendship gave me confidence when I had to survive the trauma of Angela's moving away, so that it seemed easier to find the next best friend in the fifth grade.

There were other social successes, too. I survived Girl Scout camp for a week without my parents or any close friend. True, I developed impetigo and a fever and went to bed for three days just as soon as I got home, but I was a heroine, nonetheless. I lived in those woods and slept on that cot as if I were a pioneer. In the fourth grade, I was on the Student Council and I played Queen Elizabeth I in the Elocution Recital. I was really Queen Elizabeth I when I said my lines. Total strangers came up afterwards to praise me! And in the sixth grade, my heart pounding, dressed in a beautiful dress, I was actually asked to dance twice by Paul, the boy I'd had a crush on since fourth grade. I was moving away. I couldn't know what the future held, but at that dance I was filled with a sense of elation.

I took public buses by myself and shopped in stores downtown, alone. I handled money and made decisions. So many moments, private and public, felt good! These places in my childhood were wondrous moments where I felt centered and very positive about myself, on top of the world!

Such positive Fingerprints of My Mind were not profoundly clouded by family dysfunction. Although these actual positive memories, in and of themselves, could not fortify me as an adult to become truly centered with a SONG OF MY SOUL, they are not to be dismissed. I encourage you to look for the actual memory Fingerprints in yourselves as well as in your clients.

There are other types of Fingerprints of the Mind that I'd like to discuss before I relate case examples. These are the memories of our own sense of wonderment about ourselves and about our potential, even if unactualized. These Fingerprints of the Mind involve using our imaginations – a marvelous tool at any age.

For example, I remember when I was twelve, there was a bad flood nearby. I was excited by the adventure of the flooded roads and downed bridges. I was thrilled when the Parkway behind my house was closed by damage. I wanted to help distressed victims of the flood. I knew in my heart of hearts that I could be a superior volunteer if only I would be allowed to help in the Red Cross Center in the school. I could have bandaged people and soothed them. Yes, I could literally have run the rescue center; I could have handed out blankets and cooked food and served soup; I could have stayed up all night and handled all sorts of crises if I had to. I could feel tremendous competency welling up in me. I yearned to serve.

Unfortunately, my father, who was then the superintendent of schools, did not allow me to get near the center. I felt so totally stifled, I hated him that day. Yet that healing, able, wondrous child lived on in my imagination. I was certain of her talents and her power. I knew my capabilities and how I would feel executing them. But at that time, I had no chance of living them out.

For many people, including myself, identifying this unactualized yet wondrous state of being is well worth the search. Positive energies can be drawn from the *unactualized* state of well being just as one can draw positive energies from the *actualized* self. One may have to sort through various feelings of impotence, discouragement, rage or anger such as I felt at not being allowed to do heroic work at the time of the flood, just as we therapists help our clients sort through the effects of their dysfunctional families that surround a childhood success or a moment of elation.

Positive Fingerprints of the Mind that exist in the imagination may point the way to the unactualized self and begin the process of

45

actualizing it. This was the case when my friend, Leon, dreamed about himself as a loving warrior.

Leon's dreams

In Leon's first dream, he was involved with a woman in a loving and caring way. His life felt full, complete and wholesome. On his face were the same deep scars that marked the face of his African friend from many years before, whom Leon had greatly admired for his political astuteness and power. The black man's face had been permanently scarred in the traditional ritual fashion of his tribe.

In Leon's second dream, he again had the scar marks on his own face and was living a peaceful life in which he again felt complete and connected. Leon often talks about his psychotherapy and how profoundly important it has been in transforming his life. He has been in the process of shedding many people and activities and adding new dimensions to his life and personality. His personal goal is to let go of much of his anger and find ways to live out his dream of helping people without needing to mobilize anger to accomplish his task. In his personal life, after two unfulfilling marriages, he yearns for deep connections that are permanent and loving. In his dream, he felt very much the warrior but also the peaceful, connected lover. He awoke having a vivid sense of his own potential, yet to be actualized.

A last point about Positive Fingerprints of the Mind: We should not assume that only events that happened long ago are important to retrieve. In fact, states of well being may have just occurred an hour ago, last week or last year. Clearly I'm not talking only about the wounded child. Indeed, I'm not talking about a capacity that is in any way restricted to childhood. Often it's easier to get good representations of states of elation and wholeness from childhood because childhood often lingers vividly and poignantly in our memory banks; however, we can retrieve valuable states of well-being from anytime in our lives.

A peak experience occurred for me when I was a young adult teaching twenty-seven second graders. I don't remember what the lesson was, but I remember the children being fussy and distracted. Suddenly, an idea popped into my head. I said to the class, "I have a new question to ask you: Which weighs more, a pickle or a pain?"

The children laughed and were eager to respond. Everyone seemed to have an answer. It was an easy task. I quickly proceeded to invent other questions that crossed categories, such as: "Which smells better, Christmas or Easter?" "Which would you rather be, the letter 'B' or the letter 'N'?" We had a great time and I felt a profound sense of discovery. I knew at that very moment that I'd invented a new way of linking cognition and affect. What a moment!

As we help our clients and ourselves get more in touch with our ENCHANTED SELVES- be it via exploration and affirmation of Positive Fingerprints of the Mind or Shadow Prints and/or Positive Fingerprints of The Body, we're always challenged by the following three negative dynamics:

Dysfunction surrounding a positive experience

The first impediment is the dysfunction that can lurk around positive experiences, whether actualized or imagined. A vivid example of dysfunction that interrupted the emergence of my ENCHANTED SELF happened during a ballet class when I was about twelve.

I yearned to be a dancer. I enjoyed my lessons and often felt that I had the potential to be a good dancer. One day, my ballet teacher stopped my mother as she arrived to pick me up. I overheard her telling my mother I should be discouraged from continuing dance because I was growing tall and, obviously, I would grow to be 5' 6" to 5' 8" – beyond the height permitted in professional dance! Her words penetrated like an arrow into my heart, interrupted a deep and passionate yearning that already was taking form as a goal. Although her name is lost forever in my memory, I can still see her attractive, aging body, her red hair pulled back. I can hear her French accent as she talked to my mother. That day this woman disturbed my present, as well as my future. My bubble burst. I would have to sift through my past, as an adult, to reclaim my love of dance.

Vulnerability of one's self-esteem

The second interruption to the emergence of one's ENCHANTED SELF in the vulnerability of self-esteem. It's so easy to feel diminished or threatened by a remark or criticism, as in the above example. Many, myself included, struggle with feelings of unworthiness when opportunities present themselves. Sometimes we feel as though we are a fraud and about to be exposed. Other times the possibility of public recognition of our talents is simply too overwhelming. THE ENCHANTED SELF as an enhanced state cannot emerge if we are not comfortable with ourselves. And it's not only others who spoil it for us. If we're too perfectionistic, for instance, we may be our own worst critic. Or we may carry within ourselves negative messages that make the emergence of THE ENCHANTED SELF too scary. If we are susceptible to such overwhelming anxiety, we may feel it's not worth living an enhanced life.

For example, in my teen and early adult years, my poetry and short stories were often positive releases for me. Each story or poem excited and heartened me. People told me my work was good, but more important, I knew in my heart that this was true. However, most of my creations died a dismal disenchanted death, unnourished and alone in a nameless grave (actually a locked file cabinet). I was not able to bring myself to endure the exposure necessary to go public with my work. It wasn't lack of energy. I was willing to type and send out copies of my work. What discouraged me were the wounds I experienced when rejections arrived from the first few submissions I had so hopefully sent out. Each rejection created such a grave wound that my persistence ultimately died. I felt publicly diminished. At some level I believed that a printed rejection slip really meant that my work should not be shared. Obviously my perfectionism and anxiety around public recognition interfered with my initial enthusiasm of creativity.

Self esteem as it affects the therapeutic retrieval of Positive Fingerprints of the Mind will be discussed more fully in Chapter VII.

How personal boundary violations interfere with the emergence of THE ENCHANTED SELF

The last barrier to the gradual emergence of THE ENCHANTED SELF is when personal boundaries are violated, particularly when we don't know how to get our true needs met. As a therapist as well as a woman, I've learned that women are particularly vulnerable to blurred boundaries. For one thing, we find ourselves constantly divided and conflicted by a multitude of caretaking, professional demands and other responsibilities: care of babies, of older parents, money worries and health worries are part of a modern woman's normal life. Technology adds a slew of interruptions to what could be private times: noise from television sets and telephones – even portable phones – that ring while we're reading or thinking, driving or bathing. Because of job commitments combined with housecleaning and other chores, our meals are often eaten on the run. The boundary violations of private space that most of us live with daily are so repetitive and come so naturally that after a while we don't realize how they interfere with THE ENCHANTED SELF.

Only after my own spiritual journey during these past several years did I insist that at least on Friday night, the Jewish Sabbath, the TV be turned off while we ate. The result? It's amazing how lively conversation can reenergize us at the end of a tiring week!

Helping your clients develop healthy boundaries so that their needs can be better met is a difficult part of the ENCHANTED journey and may require a long therapy. In the beginning of therapy many clients don't understand the payoff for maintaining clearer boundaries, particularly since any change in this process often results in alienating family members and close friends. Thus, treating boundary issues arouses a good deal of anxiety in clients. The good news is that most therapists are skilled in this work. I'll bring up this subject again in Chapter VII where my focus will be on how to encourage clients to realize that if they permit themselves a more clearly defined and sacrosanct space for themselves, better understanding how to get their needs met in each type of encounter, they have a better chance to restore and replenish themselves.

To summarize: the dysfunctional aspects of one's life, low self-esteem and violations of personal space all interweave to restrict the emergence of THE ENCHANTED SELF. Therapy for these problems may be long-term and difficult, arousing anxiety along the way, but is ultimately very rewarding for both therapist and client.

Separating dysfunction from potential enchanted material

I'd like to show you how you can help clients reframe and rename what they bring from their past and present to help them recognize positive states of well-being. The most essential skill the therapist employs is her listening ear, especially her ability to listen for good news amid the bad. The second skill the therapist will use is helping the client rename and/or reframe negative messages so that positive ones come to the foreground. Here are some therapeutic techniques to keep in mind when working with these skills:

1. Within past or present personal life events there may be Positive Fingerprints of the Mind, i.e., enhanced moments that the client had at one time, or is experiencing now, even if your client is too over-whelmed to acknowledge or recognize them. These moments may represent reality or they may be part of the person's imaginative life. Neither should be ignored because each has the rich potential to help our clients reorganize their capacities to live enhanced lives.

2. Keep your listening skills active rather than passive. We all occasionally anticipate a person's baggage. When we make assumptions we listen less intently. Or we hear what we want to hear, looking for confirmation of the themes we've chosen to work on with a client. This is a disservice to the client. Be patient and you may find, even well into the therapy, that she slips in a remark or comment that we can recognize as a key to unlocking her positive resources.

3. Pay keen attention to your client's whole persona. If she shifts in her chair to a more upbeat position; if you see more energy flowing through her body; if her eyes light up as she talks about a certain subject; if her voice sounds lighter, take note. You may find out what she's experiencing, even if she's not aware of it. Don't expect that she can always explain herself, but you can encourage her with your interventions: "Do you hear the change in your voice? I wonder what that means to you?" Let her come to her own conclusions about the shift you notice. If she denies a shift has taken place, let her wait until next time before pressing the point. She may resist giving up an old identity as a depressed person. Once your client acknowledges her Positive Fingerprints, make sure that you reinforce the good news. Positive feedback helps her reclaim her strengths.

50

Renaming is simply pointing out talents and other strengths that the client may scarcely recognize as belonging to herself. Reframing is a broader technique. The therapist herself helps the client achieve a perceptual shift by telling her how her strengths can be woven into her life and self image. By suggesting cognitive shifts in the way she might view herself, you weave in positive information that you have stored about her. She'll be encouraged because you remembered all this time!

Client cases

Here are two cases where clients brought up good news they'd previously ignored. I'll indicate where different listening techniques have been used and show you how I reframed and renamed their material.

Brenda

As usual, Brenda began her session talking about her parents. Even as a married adult, she was often disturbed by their disregard of her. For the second time she told me a story about how she and her husband Harold desperately needed a weekend alone at the shore. They'd requested the use of her parent's cottage a month in advance and her parents had agreed to the request. However, as the time approached, her parents called to announce that they would be joining Brenda and Harold for that weekend! Brenda felt violated. Once again, her parents had dismissed her wishes.

During a pause, I asked her to tell me how her dad, whom she saw as particularly dismissive, had been raised. Brenda described the profound disregard that her father had experienced as a little boy in a cold, judgmental family. She, by herself, came to the conclusion that this was probably why he needed to boss and dominate. I asked about her mother's family. When she talked about her mother's parents her face softened, her eyes became more luminous and, as she sat there, she seemed to bloom physically. Brenda's body language gave me all the information I needed to show that she was in touch with life-enhancing memories.

She continued, "I guess some of my best memories are tied into my mother's mother. My grandmother and grandfather were

51

immigrants who struggled to make a living. They were one of the first Jewish families to buy property in the Pocono Mountains. They had a guest house and dairy cows. Every summer we lived there with my grandparents. Those were wonderful times for me. It was there that I learned to love animals. Sometimes I was lonely, but I always had a pal – a dog or a cow or a horse – or I would watch the birds, or make friends with the chipmunks. "Even if my grandmother was occasionally neglectful of me," she went on, "I only felt really free – a good feeling – when I was visiting her. You know how I've told you that my parents never left me alone. I was constantly directed, supervised and orchestrated. But at Grandma's I would get up in the morning and go out and wander all day. (No one was afraid of kidnapping in those days.) I could wander from field to road, or go into town five miles away. Sometimes I'd go and look for my grandfather, who was a tailor and worked in the town a few days a week. I learned so many things those summers to make me feel good about myself. There were so many little things, like aromas and weather, that went with those summers. You know, it's funny, but just the other morning the weather felt to me the way it used to feel in summer then."

I responded, "I appreciate your sharing those wonderful times with me. I can see that so many of your talents stem from those childhood experiences." Brenda had already told me about her love for animals and how protective and careful she was with her three cats. She also made clear where her love of gardening had come from. Although much of her private time as an adult had been interrupted by physical illness, there were all these arenas of gratification. I believe that my comments to Brenda, illuminating the origins of some of her talents, helped her open up further.

She began to talk about her manual dexterity. Although as a child she was indifferent to dolls, she was ecstatic when someone gave her a tool box. Her grandfather was very handy with tools and she would follow him around the farm with her little tool box. She then noted the connection between her grandfather's skills and her own. Although her mother was artistic and drew, she recognized that her grandfather was more supportive of her own efforts.

I replied, "Yes, you do have a lot of manual skill. How great that your grandfather helped you learn to do so many things. Not only are you talented with your hands, but you've developed a wonderful career as a jewelry-maker." I validated and emphasized her Positive Fingerprints of The Mind as well as talents she'd expressed as an adult.

I now went on to re-frame: "I encourage you to stay in touch with these positive memories. When you feel bored or at a loss for something to do, go back to the summers on the farm in the Poconos and remember the beautiful things from your childhood. It's important to do this because all of this history you are talking about today really supports the functional, creative side of you and can help you move away from your dysfunctional entanglement with your parents. Not that we don't have to work seriously on many of your emotional issues with your parents, but the positive memories of yourself can be very life-sustaining and can reinforce you as a talented, creative adult with the strength to resolve and overcome the hurt and over-involvement you still feel with your parents."

I didn't dismiss the pain she felt around the dysfunctional parts of her life, but I suggested she give more room in her mind to her talents and positive memories. She needed to see herself as a competent adult, no longer only as the hurt child. Brenda acknowledged then that she does visit, in her own way, the good places in her life. She said, "This year I planted a lot of gladioli and I can't wait for them to come up. My grandfather used to plant them. Gladioli give me a connection with him every day."

This was an example of when a client already is connecting to Positive Fingerprints, but does not think of them as appropriate therapy material because she thinks therapy is only for "problems." Sometimes the therapist needs to give her client permission to bring in positive material. The therapist might gently point out that the client is only bringing in problems and never anything positive and ask her if she realizes she's doing this and why. The therapist can then correct the misperception that therapy is only for "bad" news.

Brenda went on to do her own work reframing her grandparents in terms of generational issues: "My grandparents were not good parents because they were obsessed by survival needs and often ignored my mother. They must have been very hurtful to her. To this day my mother carries a grudge against them. However, they were able to support the good parts of me." Thus Brenda demonstrated that she was able to be realistic about all the capacities of family members, able to separate what was positive from what was negative and destructive and see that her parents, like all people, were mixtures of good and bad qualities.

I had utilized slight shifts in focus looking for positive information from Brenda. This client was emotionally able to sort through some of her past, separating destructive from constructive influences. We didn't spend most of our time looking for Brenda's wounded child, since we already knew she'd lacked consistent emotional nourishment. Rather, by sifting through Brenda's positive memories, we both found a way to reach Brenda's talents and emotional strength, and could focus on her capacity to support herself. Brenda walked out of the room feeling high; I could tell that by her body movements. Whereas she had lumbered in, communicating the heaviness she felt, she left in an upbeat manner, moving quickly and decisively.

This case is an example of how a clinician who is practicing "THE ENCHANTED SELF" accompanies her client through a session. At first, the session appeared to be more of the same old weary tale being told just one more time, in one more version, one more chapter. Suddenly, there is a shift to more positive material within the session. Sometimes clients shift on their own and the therapist reinforces them; sometimes the therapist senses that the timing is right to look for positive material and lets the client know. This releases clients to tell their stories from a more positive perspective so that silver linings in their own memory banks appear. Suddenly, they find themselves in a new place, having previously viewed their lives as only a hardship, perhaps feeling disheartened. Given encouragement by the therapist to look for positive threads in their histories, they find more good news in themselves than they might have realized existed. The therapist enthusiastically receives the good news and reflects it back to the giver.

As I mentioned earlier, listening is a delicate art. One of the most vulnerable spots for us as clinicians is that we may become habituated to a particular client's therapy style. We no longer expect or look for good news, so we don't hear it when it comes. An example from my practice points to this vulnerability.

Maria

I'd been making every effort to help a mid-life woman see herself and her world through a more positive lens. After a bad marriage in which she was constantly criticized by her husband, she'd sought psychotherapy to help her through the divorce process. She often came in despondent, down-in-the-dumps, expressing defeat. Maria often requested advice rather than participating in any type of psychotherapeutic process. Maria had no confidence in her coping skills and very little sense of self worth. I tried to listen for whatever good news she brought up and spent a lot of my energy supporting and encouraging her to fight for a decent divorce settlement. I tried to give her positive feedback for following through on these steps.

One day Maria came in more than usually light-hearted. Rather than ask for advice, we talked. She mentioned that she had fun at Easter. She'd taken out some of the exquisite fine china and silverware that her mother had given her and set the table in a very elegant manner for herself and her eleven year-old daughter – just for the two of them. She taught her daughter how to use a napkin ring and practiced other dining manners. I knew that this was good news, but my listening skills with Maria were already weakened. I gave some positive reinforcement, but it was as if I were listening to her at the other end of a long tunnel. I barely caught an important comment she made about her life having changed since her childhood.

"Yes, my life was once incredibly different, bizarre and fascinating." Fortunately, I woke up.

"Tell me about that life, tell me more about it." My request turned out to be extremely significant. Maria told many stories of her exotic childhood, about her flamboyant, eccentric grandparents who went suddenly from riches to rags in a financial debacle. I could now better tune in to her unresolved personality issues. As I reflected on the session, I saw that much of my previous work hadn't taken into account how much she saw herself as unique because of her idiosyncratic background. All my interventions up to that point had been based on what she had told me. But it wasn't the whole story. I didn't know about the truly unusual life that Maria was trying to talk about now, and probably trying to get hold of again.

Maria needed and deserved to be understood in all aspects of her life. No one had bothered to understand her whole story, including me! Much of her depression and advice-seeking was because she'd lost a former identity that no one had recognized. A few sessions later she shared that when I had asked about her past she had thought I was just one more in the line of mental health providers who made her feel that the problems in her life stemmed from her childhood, resulting in her feeling that there was something wrong with her. I responded by saying that I was surprised but glad that she had told me this. I explained that what I had been doing in the last couple of sessions was looking for what might have been positive in her childhood. I was trying to hear her whole story, listening intently to what was beautiful and creative − although perhaps eccentric and different − about her family of origin, looking for positive messages that she could utilize in the present, as she had shared her family's customs and ceremonies with her daughter.

After Maria better understood why I was interested in her past, she continued to share more fascinating information in other sessions. In one session, she reminisced about a great grandmother who had been extremely gifted with animals. She was known in her community as the unofficial "Doc" whom people consulted if there was anything wrong with their farm animals. This information about her great grandmother tied into Maria's own love of nature and animals. There was also an uncle who had been an early photographer. Some of his work was shown in the Statehouse and the Smithsonian Institution in the early 1900s. This excited Maria because her artistic side is an important part of her.

Earlier in her therapy, she had talked bitterly about how her parents had prevented her from becoming an architect, which she felt would have combined her artistic talents with a legitimate way to make a living. She was finally able to hypothesize that her parents probably were seeing the world from their perspective and did not intentionally keep her from thriving. It was just not part of their world for a girl to study to be an architect. This insight did not remove all of her anger and bitterness, but it did help Maria understand how learned values affect the coping and judgment capacities of each person, even of parents. Finally, she was able to share her past with an "expert" without feeling that only her dysfunction was of interest.

Many clients associate retrieval work with pain and the horror of possibly exposing one's own deficits or secrets or those of one's family. It helps them to know that when you're reviewing their past you're looking for what might be positive, which I've called Positive Fingerprints. I don't think this should be a secret from your client!

This chapter has taken you through some of my reflections on the value of retrieving Positive Fingerprints of The Mind. Through my own memories as well as my clients', I've tried to give you a better understanding of the price we pay in our development and in the therapy we do when we don't fully accept or even recognize our own needs, or help our clients to accept and recognize their Positive Fingerprints. I have provided some guidelines and illustrations for listening, reframing and renaming as you work with clients. Obviously this is not so different from all clinicians' basic training, but I've tried to show why I think more work is needed and what is lost when we focus too much on pathology. In the next chapter I'll discuss the "Shadow Prints of the Mind," important positive memory traces that look a little different, clinically.

Reader's exercise

Searching for Your Positive Fingerprints of the Mind.

Please jot down your answers to the following so that you can integrate these positive memories later:

1. Much of what makes you special happened in your imagination even if your fantasies could not be actualized. Relax and let your mind wander to different areas in your life that have given you pleasure, such as nature, sports, relationships, cooking or politics. Once you have found them, search for an image that appeared in your imagination from that time. For example, perhaps you were a Brownie Scout and imagined yourself being a star Girl Scout someday, winning every badge. Or maybe, because you loved nature, you often imagined yourself climbing high up in trees. You may never have been able to actualize any of these fantasies. When you remember an unactualized Positive Fingerprints of the Mind, take a few minutes to enjoy it.

Remember how good it felt to daydream.

2. Now, at this time in your life, daydream again – imagine yourself accomplishing special things or having certain wonderful things happen to you. Try to recreate some of the delight that you had when you fantasized as a child. Try not to hold on to any disappointment or anger that resulted from unrealized dreams.

Please jot down your daydream now.

3. Now get in touch with some positive traits, coping styles, or talents that you currently have or that you can see yourself retrieving from your past. Perhaps you're still courageous, perhaps you still have boundless energy, perhaps you could still be a good athlete with the right training.

Please make a list of those now.

4. If these are unactualized, write down at least one way in which you might actualize these Positive Fingerprints of your Mind. Don't be afraid to let your imagination be your guide. For example, a course in rockclimbing might help you get back in touch with the fearlessness you felt as a child climbing trees. Later you can come back and figure out all the practical steps needed to actualize your potential embedded in your Positive Fngerprints.

Chapter Seven

Reclaiming Positive Shadows

I N chapter VI, I discussed how to recognize Positive Fingerprints of the Mind in your clients and in yourself, whether they occur in memory, reality or in the imagination. This chapter focuses on the feelings that surround a positive state of being. As your client learns to recognize subtle positive feelings that exist when she is in a positive ego state, she can figure out how to best recreate those feelings. For example, your client may have enjoyed archery as a child; she may have felt powerful and in control of her world as she shot each arrow. As an adult she may have absolutely no interest in archery, yet she can learn to enjoy feeling powerful and in control. Or she may recognize feeling "good" when she looks at a beautiful sunset, even without a particular memory attached to it. She may need encouragement to feel good and to learn how to capture for future reference those times when this feeling emerges.

In this chapter you'll learn how to help your client recognize and experience positive feelings that heighten her capacities for enhanced living. You'll need to listen carefully to your client and to yourself so that you can document an enhanced state of being and help label the feelings associated with that state. Many feelings are not easily put into words and are also so idiosyncratic that we cannot be certain exactly what another person has experienced emotionally. Autonomy in Enchanted Self therapy occurs when the client can become responsible for recognizing her own Enchanted states.

We learn to communicate with language, but so often language falls short of giving us a way to fully share with another the special feelings that we may have. How do you really share feeling "peaceful," "relaxed," "authentic," "whole," "connected," "close to God"? I imagine that many of us have stumbled around trying to communicate these profound positive states, assuming we've been lucky enough to have been there and to have recognized them.

Sensuality is also hard to express in words. How do we explain to another what cinnamon really tastes like or what the particular smell of a rose stirs up in our mind? How do we describe exactly what it is about a sunny day that makes us feel good? What does feeling "good" mean to me on that sunny day? How do I explain that honeysuckle stirs up a feeling of hope if my memory of a sense experience can't be articulated?

When we talk about subtle internal positive experiences, language may limit us from accurately capturing these states. This lack accounts for the use of music, dance, poetry and other arts to express exquisite emotions. Good feelings can be profound ones: a sense of wholeness, euphoria, a spiritual connection with God. Good feelings can also occupy a small moment of sweetness, such as enjoying a particular aroma. For those who don't have a great deal of self-regard, a good feeling may be fleeting. That's why it's so important that the clinician recognize, probe for, validate, document and reflect back the Positive Shadows of the Mind and/or Body. In this chapter, we'll focus on Positive Shadows of the Mind that emerge in the treatment room.

Why the name "Shadow Prints"?

A shadow is harder to identify than a clear image. I call Shadow Prints "Shadows" because positive feeling memories may be more elusive and harder to share than Positive Fingerprints of the Mind. For example, if a client says to you, "I remember how good I felt when I was editor of my high school yearbook," it's easy and often appropriate to see if these old talents can be reincorporated into the client's current life. It may be harder to understand, however, what "good" meant to the client. A feeling of authenticity? A sense of integrity? In order to help our client make vivid the feeling of "good" she mentioned, we will have to struggle with her to recall earlier feelings operating in her life at that time.

Tess

Here is Tess, explaining how she renewed earlier good feelings after a relationship broke up: "I had a boyfriend, David, for years, and at first he was very good for me. I was very flaky and he helped to ground me. But as the years went by, his negativity began to get me down. He never seemed able to go beyond this. He wallowed in many of the old stories that pained him. At one point, toward the end of our relationship, I suggested that we seek therapy. But he didn't want anything to do with it, saying there was nothing wrong with him. I said to him, 'Then I guess you don't care enough about our relationship to really struggle to improve it so that I'll feel more comfortable.' Soon we fought. In his rage, he shouted, 'Well, get out then.' And I did. I was thankful. I needed release and I couldn't release myself. As soon as I gave up, I was free.

"Living by myself, I felt almost immediately tuned in again to my younger self. I was happy over the smallest things. For example, I could come to your house, turn down the street and feel great pleasure just looking at the view. I've always had an artistic side and as soon as I was free again that part of me came back fully. With David, I had been trying to deny certain parts of myself, to become part of the 'establishment.' But it just wasn't working. I am who I am – that person who, as a child, made doll clothes for paper dolls and used bits of fabric to make clothespin dolls. That's what made me happy. My mother gave me antique buttons to decorate them with. I'd always loved doing things like that. Now I have a boutique, I have my art and even an art show coming up. I'm doing my own thing.

"Soon after breaking up with David, I met a fellow who wakes up with a smile on his face and doesn't ever bring me down. It's almost like a miracle. So many people just wallow in what was wrong in their early lives. I agree that people have to get more in touch with what was positive in their youth and then be true to those parts of themselves; it really worked for me."

After Tess broke up with her first boyfriend, she was able to return to a state of well being at several levels. She returned to earlier talents from her childhood her shop with her artistic creations, handmade clothing and the work of other artists. Also, in freeing herself from that relationship, she was able to "to tune into my younger self." This permitted her to enjoy again the simplest things, such as looking at the trees as she drove down a street. Her pleasure is a reawakened Shadow Print of the Mind.

Often, as mentioned in the last chapter, positive states cannot exist when the ego's boundaries are being invaded by other content and/or self-esteem difficulties. Tess's story of her old relationship is a good example of boundary violations and self-esteem blows that inhibited the emergence of her ENCHANTED SELF. Freeing herself from a man who did not have enough regard for her to work on their relationship, allowed her to once again actualize both Positive Shadows and Positive Fingerprints of the Mind. On her own, Tess was able to reclaim both. Here are some suggestions for finding our clients' and our own Shadow Prints of the Mind:

Listen for the client's wisdom

Everyone has the capacity to identify and recognize an optimal state of being or happiness. Our job is to facilitate the contact with earlier experiences of these positive states that leads to retrieval. The mutuality of experience that we may have with our client can help her heal faster and more thoroughly than if we only scrutinize and analyze. Here's an example:

Diane

Diane, a computer programmer, has been in therapy with me for a few years. A pretty redhead in her late thirties, she started seeing me after a divorce. One day Diane described a variety of problems, including how hard it was for her to relate to her parents, who although they love her dearly, have never been emotionally support-ive. Preoccupied with their health, they seem overwhelmed and don't communicate about anything else. Diane mentioned that she always finds herself emotionally tiptoeing around her parents, as she did as a child, trying to protect them from her feelings – her fears or hopes and dreams.

As Diane talked, I thought of the notion that what the client brings into the treatment room is a coded message about what's hap-pening between client and therapist. Was Diane telling me that she was tiptoeing around me, too? If so, did I contribute to this? I had to acknowledge that little of my time had been spent in appreciating her strengths. I wondered how this might be corrected without seeming to be artificial.

Diane related how her parents had hoped she would become a teacher. I asked her what her aspirations had been as a teenager. I hoped it would steer us back to her earlier self. Diane immediately started to talk about how much she, herself, had wanted to be a teacher. She wanted to help poor children in the ghetto, believing deeply that all children can grow if only they can get the right help. Her face grew intense and lively as she talked about student teaching in a poor ghetto school. Her commitment really showed. I realized that here was a woman with important dreams. She had a deep sense of purpose. I realized that by focusing on her neurotic characteristics and her anxieties and problems, as important as they sounded, I had trivialized her. When had we taken the time to acknowledge the power and the passion of her story, her life's theme?

At the end of the session, I told Diane how pleased I was to share her earlier aspirations. "I see that you're a person with a desire to have a purpose, to be helpful, to be connected." Her face just soft-ened in front of me. She lit up and said, "Yes I am. I thought maybe I wasn't that committed after I dropped my teaching ambition and got in with some bad people. After a while I began to think maybe it was just some sort of college idealism. I demeaned my own desire to have a purpose and to help people. But you're right, I have intense and genuine feelings about these things."

We ended the session mutually captivated by the fire and passion of Diane's memories. These Shadow Prints contained a sense of purpose and dedication that she'd lost and needed to find and own again for the sake of her ENCHANTED SELF, perhaps even for her SONG OF THE SOUL to emerge someday. For Diane, a life with purpose is not just a matter of finding the right fellow, or having a child before her biological clock runs out, or getting along well at the company. My hunch is that Diane had tiptoed around many people close to her, unable to express her innermost needs. In ENCHANTED SELF therapy, it was my job to connect her to a time in the past when she felt deeply about living a meaningful and committed life. Diane is a good example of a client whose Positive Shadow Prints of the Mind were covered up and even dismissed. If the therapist doesn't take the time to help her client reclaim them and reinforce them, they may remain lost.

Help the client see therapy as a place to bring in good news

Dawn

Let's listen to Dawn, a very bright woman working in the mental health field, who is recovering from a long history of abuse. She remarks: "When I first entered therapy I assumed that you only wanted to hear my problems. People don't come to you unless there is something that they need to work on, so they see themselves as deficient in some way, or they see themselves in pain. This is the way I felt as a new client. I don't know how much that had to do with my past therapy. I think somehow I also got the feeling that any of the good stuff you don't need to hear because that's what's OK about me. So the therapist doesn't see the whole person. If you're trained to "fix" them, that's the way you're going to treat the person. You know, every doctor today has a specialty, so they all look only at a part of you."

Dawn is right, so even if it's very difficult, we therapists need to reconsider the therapy we do and help the client to be a whole person in the treatment room.

She goes on: "If I give you a skewed pictured of myself, then you never see the whole person, perhaps only the worst part of me. Since

I'm training to be a therapist, I'm moved and affected by the way you've tried to help me retrieve my better self. I know what you're doing is on the right track because in my role as a social worker I find that when I come from a more positive place I get more from my clients. When I focus just on fixing what's wrong, we seem to get into a hole together.

"One of the things that helped me get a sense of what you're looking for came one night when you talked about your role as a teacher. That really helped me, because I was so used to seeing clinicians as authoritarian and totally powerful. Explaining that you were teaching me new ways of thinking was very helpful. Still, even to this day, I'll come in and not tell you the good stuff that happened to me – it won't even occur to me. I suppose you assume that I can handle it myself, so I withhold the good news. I was brought up not to talk about myself, especially not to brag. I know you're not asking me to brag, but so many old messages still get in the way.

"I think I finally know what you mean about experiencing THE ENCHANTED SELF. Something happened to me just tonight before I came to therapy. I like to walk on the beach. Tonight was a particularly gorgeous night. There was a full moon, it was extremely bright and the waves were rough but not dangerous or scary. It was exciting. I wanted to stay there but I couldn't because it was late. I began to walk away and suddenly I turned around. I wanted to watch the moon on my way back, but the moon wasn't there. You know how the moon follows you, so I walk again and it's behind me and again I just had to watch it. I permitted myself to walk slowly back out on the jetty and something clicked – the awe! It was like feeling adrift, like being immersed in nature, or being connected to the whole world. It was a wonderful feeling and I didn't have to do anything – I just felt whole. And then I noticed that I was standing still!

"I really couldn't process the things you said before, but now they finally clicked in. I knew I'd been there when I was younger. I used to walk along the beach in the early morning at my aunt's house. In childhood there were times when I felt serene, but as an adult, I felt too constrained. This time, though, the things you had said were in the back of my brain. I walked onto the jetty because I wanted to and the next thing I knew, I had this sense of fullness."

Dawn's transcript gives us a sense of how much permission a client may need to reach a point where she'll allow Positive Shadow Prints of her mind to emerge. Although sophisticated and insightful, until she felt my permission to tell the whole story, good as well as troubling, Dawn still withheld good news both inside and outside the therapy room. I'm sure she was also helped by my telling her about some of the concepts behind THE ENCHANTED SELF. When her breakthrough came, she experienced a profound sense of wholeness, retrieving, as she described, visual memories and emotions. When Dawn becomes a therapist, she'll be able to take her whole self into the therapy room and use her knowledge of positive memories to augment the therapy she will do.

Marsha

Marsha was a client who thought she had no Positive Fingerprints of The Mind or Positive Shadow Prints. A client in individual therapy, as well as in my women's group, she had been seeing me for several years. She entered therapy after leaving a marriage filled with physical abuse, culminating in her husband's attempt to push her down a flight of stairs. She considered herself a food addict, tracing her excessive eating back to a childhood of benign neglect. The youngest of four sisters, Marsha, on returning from school, was often given Oreo cookies and sent out to play on the back porch. Her mother, a compulsive housekeeper, was emotionally unavailable to her children.

Hearing me talk in the women's group about the ENCHANTED SELF concept, Marsha asked me to help her look for some positive places within her own memory bank. She said that her childhood appeared to her like one gray blur of parental indifference. She also recalled her parents' fights and her father constantly criticising her mother. One of the clearest messages she received in childhood was, "Don't ask." In other words, a good child is a quiet child, seen but not heard. Have a cookie and get lost.

I suggested that she interview her sisters to see if they remembered any positive childhood moments that she may have forgotten. She did interview one sister who remembered protecting Marsha as the youngest, but little else. While each girl had been shunted off and disregarded, Marsha, as the youngest, was probably the most ignored of all. Her sister, Karen, triggered a lot of anger in Marsha around these memories. Marsha related how her parents were reluctant to offer even practical advice when she was about to be married, although most parents would have considered her future husband to be a poor choice since he'd already been married twice and was supporting two young children and a child in college!

I suggested that one of her tasks as an adult woman was to give herself permission to ask questions that would help her develop better judgment. I reminded her that as adults, we're able to get in touch with positive states of mind when our decision-making produces beneficial effects. Marsha agreed. I said, "I think you are already breaking away from that inhibiting message, 'Don't ask,' by asking for help in retrieving positive parts of yourself. You're working through your feelings around dismissal, which will permit you to develop better communication skills with everyone." I then suggested, "Let's spend a little more time today searching for some of your earlier enhanced life spaces. Perhaps we can come in by a different door. Rather than looking for exact memories, let's look for more subtle retrievals, such as aroma, or perhaps a color that you liked, and see what they might bring to mind. Any of your senses may hold the memory gateway to earlier Enchanted Moments, music or sounds."

At this remark, Marsha's face lit up. She burst out, "Yes, definitely, singing! Now that was something that gave me great joy growing up. My father was very good at it. He was always performing. He used to be in the local theater and I would sometimes help with the props and getting ready for the shows. Also, we would sing as a family. I remember sitting around the kitchen table singing at meal-times. But the only problem was that my mother would sing off key. We all had good voices, except Mom. She really had a lousy voice. My dad would criticize her in front of all of us. It kind of spoiled everything."

I replied, "You must have felt awful hearing your dad criticize your mom and having the good mood spoiled. But it's still wonderful that the family was able to sing together. You see, we can sort out the dysfunctional aspects of your dad criticizing your mom in front of the children and still be left with something beautiful! Do you sing at all, anymore?"

Marsha responded, "Oh, yes, I sing with my girls all the time. We sing in the car and we're so good that one of us can sing three notes and the others can guess the song and join in. Often, we do that at suppertime. We really have a lot of fun and in church they sing like angels. I'm proud every Sunday!"

My comment to Marsha was, "It's possible that you're not giving enough importance to the good times that you're already having. It seems like you have captured something warm and joyous and from your past – something that expresses real talent. Even though there were problems in the way your father handled singing at the table, you're having a lot of fun singing as a grownup with your girls. And you have made a generational correction by not criticizing! One of the things I'm trying to teach is that we all have to work at separating the dysfunctional from the good parts of what happened to us in the past."

Marsha replied, "I should pat myself on the back more. Once in a while some feelings or sensations arouse me, some memories that seem to be positive, but they're very fleeting. I guess I should write them down because they're so subtle I forget them."

I agreed that it was important that Marsha look for more positive experiences from the past and present. Unfortunately, like Marsha, most of us are too good at observing the negative about ourselves. As a child, Marsha was not given a chance to acknowledge and recognize positive states of being. Because she was dismissed and usually ignored by her parents, she didn't receive validation from them for her own positive moods. She did remember some good moments as a child, such as sitting on the back porch eating after school. However, these memories were contaminated by the obesity problem that consequently developed and by feelings of rejection when her mother sent her outside with the cookies, to eat alone.

Other moments that contained kernels of Enchantment, such as singing together with her family, were lost because of the negative input from her father's criticality and perhaps by her mother's co-dependency. Therefore, by adulthood she'd lost her best moments of

Positive Fingerprints of the Mind, or Shadow Prints. Appropriately, Marsha was angry when she realized that she was left with her eating disorder, and sad as she recalled not being able to ask for the time she needed with her mother.

Points to remember in helping clients to access Shadow Prints

1. The clinician must be alert to the presence of old inner messages that restrict her client from getting in touch with good feelings from the past. We saw that Marsha carried within her an old message that she was not to ask questions. This restriction, internalized, kept her from assertively asking for the information she needed to make good decisions.

2. Clients need to know how to separate out dysfunction and save what was beautiful from the past, and then they must appreciate the potential power of those moments. Marsha had done some of that intuitively, but my explicit explanation was validating and informative for her.

3. The therapist should encourage clients to record and look for subtle memories and sensations that gave them pleasure or helped them to feel whole – even if they are as small as the smell of lilacs or honeysuckle. Often these subtle memories and sensations serve as keys or gateways to remembering an earlier sense of well being.

As I noted in the beginning of this chapter, most people don't have access to language that describes subtle positive feelings such as pleasure, contentment, or fullness. Clients may struggle with articulating them for a number of reasons. They may not have any idea of the inner barriers they experience when they try to communicate these abstractions. A spouse or other significant person may inhibit the expression of deep feelings, making fun of them or trivializing them, as people often do with beautiful thoughts or poetry.

4. Ask your clients to write to you. This can be a release for those who have trouble with the spoken word. One client, who had a great deal of difficulty expressing her thoughts and feelings aloud,

69

wrote them down at my request. This is what she wrote: "I have a great deal of trouble putting my thoughts and feelings into words. Often, when I experience an emotion such as happiness, contentment, love or frustration, I can't come up with the words I need to express the emotion. Instead of having the words I need, I get what I think of as 'gut' feelings. Sometimes it is a feeling inside me, sometimes it's an image of colors, sometimes it's a safe feeling when all my tension goes — at least for a moment. For instance, near my house is a road that has trees planted on both sides, forming a canopy over the street. My family calls this the 'tree tunnel.' In summer, when all the leaves are out, it's a cool, dim place. In fall, the leaves are beautiful. In either season, as soon as I enter the tree tunnel, I look around and my muscles relax. I take deep breaths and I feel peaceful. Sometimes it seems as though the feeling I get is like the aura around aliens in sci-fi movies. It's a soft focus sort of glow that wraps around the aliens. The way that soft focus glow looks is the way I picture my feelings looking, if they were visual. But I have no words that can describe the feeling — what exactly it is or how I feel because of it. 'Happy' or 'peaceful' or 'contented' just aren't expressive enough.

I've recently realized that certain music brings on these types of feelings, especially if I sit and listen with earphones and block out everything else. Sometimes it's just getting into the sounds, flying back and forth between the instruments and the voices, and sometimes it's the emotions of the music and words. Saying, 'I feel intense' or 'this really sounds incredible' is just not enough. I want to find some words to express the intensity of the feelings.

Smell also plays a part in my feelings, usually good feelings. A certain smell can trigger a happy feeling, a peaceful feeling, a contented feeling … I always feel as if there is much more inside me that needs to come out and never does, or does so slowly that it's barely noticed …"

My clinical intervention was simply giving this client permission and encouragement to write to me. Her struggle to put into words some of the beautiful and profound feelings she wants to share speaks for itself. How many of your clients, or you, yourself, have secret, untapped places within? How many of us yearn to share, if only we knew how?

Cynthia

In conclusion, let me share some insights from Cynthia, one of the women I interviewed. I had a chance to catch up with her a year after her initial interview. At that time, I gave her an update on some of my research with women as well as my clinical work. I told her I was determined to help others learn how to find their Enchanted Selves. Cynthia became very excited and said, "It was just like my wall." At first, I didn't understand what she meant. She explained that she visualizes looking at a wall in her house. On that wall she sees the various things she knows to be true. One of her images is of herself. She knows that her assignment in life is to be reflecting. In fact, the name Cynthia means reflection. Also, she was born under the sign of Cancer, which is the sign of the moon; and the moon reflects light from the sun. She sees herself as having a role of reflecting for others what they need to see. However, she can only do this well when she is clear. When she looks at her face sometimes, she knows exactly how it should look in her reflecting moments. She knows how she feels inside when she is exactly in that state. It is as if her bones feel "lined up." When she pulls away from her state of clarity, when she moves toward a negative self-message, such as when she has to rush somewhere, she's no longer a reflecting mirror to others. Then she's all jagged like a broken mirror. She feels that when she can be in that reflective state, she's at her best.

I commented to Cynthia that, indeed, she seemed to be telling me her true ENCHANTED SELF. Cynthia went on to say that this was very private language that she was now sharing. She said that my initial interview did not elicit enough comfort to speak this way. Now, in this second meeting, where I was sharing so much about my own growth and excitement, she felt more comfortable. She now found herself naturally sharing personal information with me.

This second interview with Cynthia shows not only a deeply enhancing state of well-being that she is able to reach (and, when there, is able to assist others), but it gives us important information about the complexity of sharing. Not only do people have private states of enhancement that they guard and would not dare to disclose, but many of these states are profoundly integrated and one

71

might say even mystical as they are experienced. It is a gift of the heart that they give when they allow us into such private places.

As we listen to Cynthia's explanation of when she feels a great sense of her purpose in life, or as she said, her "assignment," we hear her utilizing idiosyncratic sensations and images. She also accesses unique, private visualizations. She's aware at a very deep level when her negative impulses pull her away from feeling centered, e.g., she knows when she is in an Enchanted state and when she's not!

We need to remember that people have private and unique ways of achieving Enchanted states of well-being. I don't pretend to be teaching you all of the components involved. As you can see from Cynthia's account, there is still some magic and mystery to her capacities. And, of course, that is what originally excited me when I interviewed the women, as well as why I chose the title THE ENCHANTED SELF. In the next chapters, I'll show how we can help our clients work on self-esteem problems and boundary issues, to access their Enchanted Selves.

Reader's exercises

1. Line up five different objects with strong scents. You might include several spices, perhaps a perfume, a piece of fabric, a flower, or a food. Now slowly pick up each object, close your eyes and take in the aroma. As you savor it, let your mind drift back in time. Does the aroma arouse any positive memories for you? If you come across a clear memory, please describe it. If you come up with a general impression, such as feeling good in childhood, or feeling healthy, write that down. Take your time and enjoy whatever positive memories are aroused.

2. If you remembered something from earlier times, what were the feelings that went with this actual memory? Is there a state of being at the feeling level that you could put into words that go with this memory, such as contentment or integrity or bliss? If so, write the feeling or feelings down. If you did not have a clear memory, did any of the smells arouse within you a state or condition that you can put into words, such as feeling healthy or feeling good? Please jot that down as well.

3. In the best of all worlds, imagine how one of the positive feelings you captured about yourself in Exercises 1 and 2 could be restored or integrated with your current life. What would you need to have happen? For example, if you thought about the sense of peacefulness, can you now imagine what you'd need in your world today to get to a more peaceful state more often? Don't be afraid to take risks and let your mind go in this exercise. If you don't know what you would need to get to this state, stay with me. The chapters that follow on self-esteem and boundary issues may help you.

Chapter Eight

How Positive Self-Regard Facilitates the Emergence of THE ENCHANTED SELF

In Chapters VI and VII, I shared with you some ways to retrieve Positive Fingerprints of the Mind and Positive Shadow Prints of the Mind. We saw ourselves as possessing a kaleidoscope of positive potential. We saw that we have the capacity to behave in a variety of ways using unique combinations of talents and styles. Client histories illustrated how positive talents and approaches to life from the past can be integrated into a more enhanced self in the present. We see that to help ourselves and others retrieve Positive Fingerprints and Positive Shadows of the Mind, we must constantly pluck good news from bad. We must help ourselves and our clients to accurately label positive traits, talents, habits and sensations. Why? Because, as noted, one's past is a mix of negative and positive experiences. Often we remember painful situations too vividly and are unable by ourselves to recognize or acknowledge our own successes. We see ourselves through a mirror darkly, unable to recognize our own special qualities and their potential for reinventing ourselves more positively.

This chapter is about self-esteem, an issue that most of us have had to cope with many times in our lives, if for no other reason than because we were raised and live in a society that often devalues everything but achievement as measured by money or social power.

Despite our work on ourselves, some of us are still burdened with a negative self-image that is easily bruised or makes us vulnerable to bouts of depression. Others of us may be over-achievers who feel disappointed with ourselves – never satisfied, even though we are driven to our next achievement. Others, often women with low self-esteem, feel vulnerable and fear rejection. This makes them unable to properly negotiate from a position of strength in a relationship, sometimes even with their own children.

Struggling with a diminished sense of self worth, we may find that we can't treasure our most precious positive characteristics. As a clinician, I realize that when self-esteem is low, as it usually is in new clients, they often distort what needs to be worked on. Sometimes they're self-critical about traits that really don't need any work. Other times they may have significantly exaggerated an area that does need some development, but not as much as they think. How many clients enter treatment because exaggerated negative self dis-tortions have led to self-fulfilling negative prophecies? Rather than seeing themselves as basically "OK," with a few areas that need work, these clients come in certain that their personhood is profoundly damaged. They bring with them notions that they are not worthy of the good things in life.

Placing positive self-regard in societal perspective: my psychologist friend

While visiting my friend, Katherine, a psychologist and artist, I heard her mention that she found herself moving away from her research and writing projects. She found herself spending time within her home, doing very private things that other people might never know, acknowledge or have any interest in if they did know. She had been doing some arranging, taking her childhood dolls and doll furniture and setting them on shelves in very special ways that had meaning to her. She said, "I envy you that you are working on your book. I'm doing this strange stuff that's not public at all." I replied, "It's not strange at all. You're really doing the type of private integra-tive work that we should all do, that our country has discouraged and devalued, making us feel that things have no value unless they're public. In Judaism, there is a mystical notion that every positive act is important even if it's done totally privately and never seen by another. If it is a positive act, then it is to the good somehow! Obviously, the act of putting your dolls in order and setting them up is good for you. Maybe it helps you feel connected to good feelings about your past, your mother – maybe it enables you to experience some private, secret space."

Katherine said, "I like listening to what you're saying. It is so sad about our culture that we haven't helped people prepare themselves for any sense of private success, that all success is public."

Later on, when I happened to notice accidentally the four shelves that had the dolls and doll furniture on them – all from the 1950's, I saw how beautifully set up they were. Each shelf looked like a little house in itself. One shelf had a television, another had a full kitchen setup. Each shelf was very much alive. They had beauty and structure. The little dolls looked so happy. I wanted to hang out there and look and look and look. I thought to myself that Katherine must indeed thrive in a very personal private space that others would not necessarily fully comprehend or be a part of. I began to think about what keeps someone like Katherine or, for that matter myself, from recognizing the self-worth of private time and private successes, no matter how personal, and idiosyncratic they may be.

My sense is that both self-esteem and boundary issues are interwoven into this lack of recognition of private successes. We're taught that our self-value is reflective of how well we are doing in terms of the outside world – how pretty we are, how bright we are, how competitively well we do in sports, how many children we have, how successful they are, what kind of house we can afford to buy, how many cars we have, what awards we receive, etc. All of these are external measures. We need to develop a sense of self-worth that is a personal capacity for positive self-regard that comes from within. To achieve this internalized capacity for self-regard, one needs a loving and supportive childhood where one has experienced nurturant, adequate parenting. One also needs a society that supports and encourages appropriate boundaries along with a sense of personal worth that is not completely reflective of external achievements and successes.

Consequently most of us have not internalized a rich sense of privacy and the worth of private time. After all, the personal habits, no matter how bizarre, of celebrities and ordinary people are disclosed continuously on television and other media. In addition to being competitive, our culture encourages the most superficial voyeuristic interest rather than an in-depth sharing and empathy. One comes home and immediately puts on television or the radio. The bombardment of stimuli continues, whether it is from the music on the stereo or from the next rented video. Even when people get together to converse, background noise of a newscaster or a video game intrudes. Space and time are not often regarded as sacred dimensions, which although they may be temporarily empty, are still available for new interpersonal experiences, or are places where private thoughts and feelings can be birthed.

That was Katherine's challenge. She sings her SONG OF THE SOUL much of the time. She has displayed her art work; she has published articles; she has given poetry readings; she is an accomplished psychologist. Yet she couldn't give herself full validation for time spent in private pursuits that would not be reflected in the public at any level. Such self-diminution left her feeling ambivalent about what was really a necessary part of her personal replenishment agenda. At some level this ambivalence would restrict the full singing of her SONG OF THE SOUL.

My struggle with positive self-regard

Listening to Katherine reminded me of many of my own self-esteem issues. My cousin Claudia was so beautiful. When I was five and she was six, we stood together in front of the mirror. Her shining hair framed her face, straight, rich and auburn red. Her skin was ivory, her cheeks had a peachy cast and her blue eyes flashed. She was perfect. In the mirror I saw my face as wispy, my skin looked sallow and blotchy and my hair was messy. Somehow I was less solid, I felt less "perfect" than my cousin.

This internalized perception was often reinforced, perhaps innocently, by my Aunt Ruth, Claudia's mother, who would sometimes comment on my messy hair or clothing, or by my mother, who would comment on Claudia's beauty. The distortion continued even into adulthood. Even now, I can look into the mirror and somehow feel not as I wish to be. I need my hair and my makeup to be "just so." I don't do well on a "bad hair day." Although as a child I loved to dance and move and be active, from that point on I took as my reference point the comparison with Claudia. My looks only please me, even now, as I approach Claudia's "perfect" look. Because of the initial distortion in self-perception at age six, I then distorted other aspects of my physical self as a young child. I hated my slightly plump thighs, my hair and the dark circles under my eyes from my allergies. My external physicality took on a negative cast.

Family dysfunction mixed with my distortion of self-image, a dysfunctional pattern that I wasn't responsible for. My parents had encouraged too much inactivity, because of anxiety about my health. I really wanted to move and dance and run. I craved activity. I was all motion. My mother shunned running, bicycling, skating, or sledding. To her, these activities were potentially lethal. (She had had three serious accidents as a young child. One accident, at age three, involved being dragged by the fender of a milk truck, by her upper lip!) If I performed these activities, I might fall and hurt myself! Although I insisted on learning how to ride a bike and learning how to swim (my dad taught me both activities), the sense of dread remained with me. When I was little, most of my mother's energies went towards protecting my health. She did an admirable job, taking me to doctors and providing the right food and medicines, while my father invested most of his emotional energies into giving me a sense that I was highly intelligent. Certainly, feeling intelligent fed my self-esteem. But I felt intuitively that my father had wished for a boy rather than a girl, and that feeling undermined my sense of self. Mother's preoccupation with my health and welfare, her devotion to me, gave me a sense of being loved and being "precious", but her inability to fully respond to physical activity left me struggling for a role model.

The same year that I looked longingly at Claudia in the mirror, I twisted my ankles three times, my right ankle twice and my left once. Each incident resulted in weeks of foot-soaking, wearing bandages and hobbling to school. My physical nature was not getting a chance to flourish. At the critical ages of five and six, I was becoming encased in a non-athletic body. Although certain corrections were made later in childhood by sheer will, such as teaching myself to ice skate even though for months my ankles literally lurched every time I attempted to walk on ice, I still responded to all the external cues of the late '50s and early '60s. Beauty was a quality women added onto themselves via puffy hairdos, lipstick, mascara, crinolines and high heels. Deep inside I knew that there was a way to feel beautiful that was more profound. I knew this way involved movement and a natural sense of one's body. However, it was so hard to hold on to this enhanced sense of my physical being. It was way down a long tunnel of poodle skirts, pointed shoes and padded bras.

Like the young child who intuitively knows a situation is immodest or inappropriate, but is helpless to control it, as Manis Friedman discusses in *Doesn't Anyone Blush Anymore?*[17] I intuitively knew that my self-esteem in terms of my physical nature had suffered an unnatural blow. I had been violated by caring adults' dysfunctional perceptions and by society's dysfunctional standards. It would be many years before the innocent person who loved her body as well as her mind could find a harmonious connection between them. There is an African expression, "It takes an entire community to raise a child." Certainly for me, positive ownership of my mind and body required the help, guidance and support of many people over many years.

How I developed positive self-regard

Among those who were able to communicate their positive regard for me were Del Sylvester and Dr. Alice B. Crossley. I met Mr. Sylvester, then seventy, when I was sixteen. He died only four years later. A self-educated humanitarian, he loved people, animals, nature and democracy. He befriended my entire family and found a special way to relate to each of us. To my mother, who loved gourmet food, he sent recipes and menus of his meals when he was traveling abroad. He talked about school politics with my dad, who was the superintendent of schools. Eagerly he attended Board of Education meetings to keep up with my father, and offered whatever advice he could. He dignified my philosophical bent by enthusiastically engaging me in deep discussions as well as by sending me philosophical letters. He constantly applauded my capacities for growth and my attempts to understand profound truths. Most important to me he, uniquely, encouraged my physical nature by buying me my first set of skis. No warnings of turned ankles from him! He encouraged me to live, to grow and thrive. He supported marriage and family life, but cautioned me not to marry too young. I know he saw the innocence, not the corruptibility, within me. I've never forgotten his love of me and our family. His portrait has hung on my bedroom wall for my entire marriage. My husband never knew Mr. Sylvester, but he quickly understood his significance to me.

Dr. Alice B. Crossley was my dissertation advisor at Boston University. She recognized my creativity and encouraged me to become a teaching fellow under her tutelage. Dr. Crossley gave me leeway in developing a dissertation topic that merged education and psychology, resulting in a case study analysis of the use of metaphorical thinking to enhance creative thinking in children. She taught me how to teach at the college level, rewarded me with praise and encouragement, and saw the creative potential of my mind.

My Judaic studies permitted me a sense of positive self-regard in which I could begin to practice honoring myself without relying on external recognition. Shelia Kongsberg, in *Holy Days: The Life of a Hasidic Family*, states, "A lot of what we do is done in private, but in our lives 'private' does not mean 'inferior'."[18] Reading this, I could begin to understand what she meant. In a world where each moment is sacred, where the goal in human development is to bring sacredness into all tasks, whether private or public, one does not need external recognition, i.e. achievement, success, money, winning, or some other measurable reward. In a world where a private act can have validity, meaning and joy even if only experienced by yourself, a whole new dimension of self-regard begins to open. I have tasted that world. But I have also experienced enough violations and disappointments in our competitive society to wish to continue on a personal journey toward a self-regard that is enriched from an inner wisdom that speaks louder than the amplified external world.

Reflections on myself as a client in terms of developing positive self-regard

In thinking about my own struggle with poor self-esteem, I wondered why my own experiences with psychotherapy had not been

81

fully restorative in terms of my sense of self and my sense of worth as a person. Let me be clear: I'm not dismissing or diminishing my psychotherapy. Without it I couldn't have accepted, at a deep, integrative level, the good news about myself given to me by other people, experiences and opportunities. However, there was one factor missing at times in my therapy, which was not missing in any of these other positive experiences or in the attitudes of those most significant to me. What was missing was a sense of hope and belief in me and my positive potential. There were too many times when my flaws seemed bigger than life.

When Mr. Sylvester befriended me, there was never a conversation or a letter from him that did not reinforce his belief in me and my capacities to thrive as an adult. Dr. Crossley, too, made clear to me the positive expectations she had of me. Because of that, even her constructive criticisms did not break my optimism. As I described in Chapter IV, my Judaic studies have given me a sense of hope about myself, as well. Mrs. S., my Torah teacher, was able to transmit a sense of joy and privilege in knowing me, just as I feel in knowing her.

Taking positive self-regard back to the treatment room

When we enter the therapy room we often feel down and defeated, like a bird with a broken wing, overwhelmed, out of our element, frightened, confused, emotionally tired. Our vulnerability becomes the therapist's challenge; intimate information is given to the therapist, then interpreted by her and shared in a way that can expose long-hidden and guarded defense mechanisms and secrets. It is true that there is an invasion of privacy, but like the surgeon's knife, this invasion can be life-saving. But let's acknowledge how vulnerable the client feels in the process. My therapists did indeed see my potential and my talents. They often pointed both out to me when I didn't see them or reassured me that I could accomplish my goals. They reinforced, supported and encouraged me. However, I was not always able to experience a sense of positive regard from them that would have meant to me, "I like you just the way you are." They felt they needed to point out to me aspects of myself that I was unable to process without a sense of personal diminishment.

As therapists, we have an obligation to provide a totally positive environment filled with acceptance, positive regard, hope and optimism. How we can do this and at the same time give important feedback, some of which is negative and painful, is the delicate art of walking a tightrope of responsibility.

Creating a self-enhancing environment in the treatment room

As therapists, we need to watch for every possible opportunity to offer the client positive regard, a sense of hope and optimism, rather than dwell on characterlogical "flaws" (really, dysfunctional behavior). These can be pointed out and worked on as necessary, but even maladaptive behaviors can be looked at in a context of untapped potential in a positive frame of reference. When a person is in pain, she may actually forget her achievements, hopes, dreams, capabilities and talents. Her sense of self worth may have de-escalated dramatically as more and more negative self perceptions developed – a common phenomenon during stressful life events. One may be feeling guilty or depressed, or both, and may have lost perspective on what is valuable about one's self.

We need to stay aware that our clients bring to us what's troubling them, but important as that is, this is not necessarily all of who they are or what their potential is. Seeing the client only at the moment when she's in the throes of worries, despair, mood changes or defensive reactions is like watching a mule carrying a too-heavy pack – its movements show how it moves up hill under an unbelievable weight. This is not how it behaves while carrying a normal load! Although focusing on the search for pathology may be appropriate for many related medical fields, it is often the opposite of what can be helpful to the client looking for mental health assistance. As Abraham S. Twerski comments in his book, *Let Us Make Man*, "In the case of emotional or behavioral problems incident to a negative self-image distortion, the usual medical approach is ineffectual and may even be counter productive. The patient's difficulties are not due to what is wrong with him but, to the contrary, they are consequences of his not being aware of what is right with him."[19]

We need to harness whatever self-esteem our client possesses so that the work of the psychotherapeutic process can begin. No one has much energy to work after hearing "bad" news about oneself. To catalogue the client's failures and "problems" will only leave her feeling depressed. Many a client hasn't returned for more after such a first session.

Suggestions for therapists

1. The treatment room is a powerful place. As noted, the client usually enters in a vulnerable emotional state. Because of this, she may exaggerate negative feedback from the therapist. Information from your client that counters her negative self-image will need to be teased out and reinforced many times. As earlier taught in Chapters VI and VII, the clinician must constantly search for and acknowledge Positive Fingerprints of the Mind as well as Positive Shadows of the Mind. Try to encourage and acknowledge the dreams and hopes for your client that emerge in treatment. In terms of improving self-esteem as well as encouraging the self, the clinician should look for ways to point out successes, functional capacities and future potential. Help her separate the dysfunctional aspects of her past from the functional, so that she can confirm her own strengths rather than weaknesses.

2. Use clinical interventions and teaching methods to bolster the client's self-esteem. These methods include renaming and re-framing as well as supportive techniques such as encouragement, a sense of reciprocal involvement, concern and sincere interest.

3. Point out functional aspects of the client's personality rather than the pathological aspects. Have the courage to sit on information you've documented about pathology. See if you can find a way to interweave it as "good news," rather than have the client hear it as incriminating information. Don't forget that most clients who experience self-esteem deficits have superegos ready and waiting to beat

them up unmercifully with any negative information they receive about themselves from another, certainly from a therapist whom they already see as an authority figure.

Case studies

I've seen two common patterns of self-esteem issues in my clients:

1. The client who is easily wounded by others and is extremely sensitive to criticism.

2. The client with a deeply internalized negative sense of self. These two of course overlap.

Any of us who have internalized negative self-messages are also sensitive to criticism from others.

Similarly, those who are very sensitive to criticism are more likely to turn these criticisms into negative self-messages. Here are case studies from each pattern.

Wounded by criticism: Rose

Rose said, "Sometimes I still think about my marriage and the pain wells up inside of me. I don't understand how I was so taken by George. Was I so hungry for love and marriage that the love poems he wrote to me convinced me I wanted to be with this man for the rest of my life? He tricked me. He was so sweet and appealing while we were courting. He chased me. 'I want to be with you all the time,' he would say. I didn't realize that he wanted me at his beck and call. It wasn't until after we were married that he began to make me feel stupid. Whenever I would have an idea, he would say, 'That and a nickel will get you a cup of coffee,' or his other favorite expression, 'Good intentions pave the way to hell.' He would actually say to me, 'You're ugly and you're stupid, therefore, you have to stay with me'. After a while I began to believe him. Looking back, I don't know how I finally gathered the strength to lock the doors that one last time and slip out with our two children to my parents' before he came home. Perhaps it was the swollen ankle from the night before when he had pushed me down three steps. I don't know exactly, but I left.

"And here I am now, six years later, alone in a small apartment with two little girls, no money, living paycheck to paycheck and doing a job I hate. I haven't had a date, I'm lonely in many ways. I'm forty years old, my hair is getting grey and I'm fifty pounds overweight. Where am I going? I want to move forward but I'm disgusted."

I responded, "But Rose, look how far you've come. What a sign of strength that you were able to leave! He was an overwhelmingly negative, dominating figure. He broke your spirit, he broke your self-esteem, he made you feel stupid and without any options in life. In a sense you were a prisoner. I so much admire your courage to leave and take life one tiny step at a time. You found a way to live by yourself with your girls; you found a way to earn some money and have the dignity of your own apartment. You've met some friends. It's true you haven't dated, but you've been preoccupied with taking care of your children and running your household. There's only so much energy any of us have available. Do you think you're ready to venture any farther at this time? Do you want to date?"

Rose responded, "I don't think I'm really ready for that yet. I do think I'm ready to use a baby-sitter on Saturday night and to make definite plans with friends. I'm also ready to take a little better care of myself. I thought about taking up yoga and perhaps walking at lunch. I really let my body go over the years, giving into excessive eating when I was nervous. I want to try new things. My neighbor said she'd help me dye my hair in exchange for me baby-sitting for her little boy a couple of Sunday mornings a month."

I replied, "That sounds really good. You seem to have some areas you want to work on. Beginning to reclaim your own body is certainly a major step toward considering another intimate relationship. I know how important it is for you not to be swallowed by a relationship again. It seems to me that socializing with other singles and taking care of your appearance are good steps."

None of the above information from Rose was new. This time, however, she wanted to reframe her story in a way that would permit growth. During her three years in therapy, we worked on her obsessive thinking centered around negative memories of her marriage and her anger towards her ex-husband. We also discussed practical matters about the two little girls, who had suffered major adjustment problems. Later in her therapy we worked on fortifying her self-esteem as a job-hunter, managing a bank account, etc. The therapy had been practical, supportive and, at times, insight-oriented. Most crucial, I seized every opportunity to communicate to Rose the sense of positive regard and respect that I genuinely felt for her.

There were several results from the session above. One was that Rose did, indeed, begin to respect her body more. One day she told me she'd walked twenty minutes at lunchtime every day that week. Soon after, Rose signed up for a weight-reduction program. While she'd been this route many times, dropping out after despairing episodes of "failure," this time she seemed more ready to take the weight loss slowly and not be as punitive to herself when she slipped up. She was proud of a very slow loss followed by periods of stabilization and/or slight weight gains. I saw my job to be non-critical, encouraging, always teaching compassion and understanding to counteract her tendency to self-criticize. I was consistently supportive. Rose told me it helped her when I taught her steps in the recovery process. I reminded her that she had been under tremendous strain – emotional, physical and financial – for many years. I explained that very often people don't put their health or bodies in order until they've taken care of some of their emotional trauma.

Several months later, Rose came back to therapy looking bright and almost like the cat that had swallowed the canary. She reported that she'd had an interesting week of flashbacks to happy times earlier in her life. She talked about her college days and some of the good times she once had. When she casually reminisced about a fellow she had dated before she met her husband, her eyes sparkled. Intuitively, I suspected that Rose wanted to talk about some of her earlier relationships, perhaps some in which she had felt more validation as a human being and as a woman than she had with her husband. I asked her to tell me a little more about this romance. She said she'd enjoyed his company in every way. They'd been engaged, but it was almost a mild boredom that led to their breaking up. Rose had some regrets about the break-up, in view of her marriage to George. She said, "My life would have been very different if I had married Neil. He'd have treated me very well."

Rose then went on to talk about how empty her life was at forty, compared to those happy days with Neil. But she said, "At least I'm going back to those happy times and thinking about them rather than obsessing about all the bad times with my husband."

I said I thought this shift in focus was a hopeful sign in her development. If she'd had happy times before she could have them again. Of course, we still had work to do so that she'd no longer be troubled by the intense discouragement she still talked about, but I wasn't worried. Rose had come a long way and I told her so. "You've walked down a long, long tunnel and now you're coming toward the light at the end of the tunnel. It's a good sign that you're looking back at what felt good and reasonably workable rather than just focusing on the negative."

During this session, I intuited that Rose was attempting to reclaim her female sexual spirit. She wasn't dating and she was dissatisfied with her looks and age, but she allowed herself the pleasure of recollecting a former positive relationship with a young man and the joy that surrounded it. It was time to hear the story and enjoy it with her. By recounting those memories while I actively listened, her sexuality seemed to awaken.

Two weeks later, Rose came in excited. She wanted to learn yoga. She'd done some in college and wanted to get back to it as a way of taking care of her health and reducing stress. She brought with her a magazine that listed local yoga classes. We had a mutually enthusiastic conversation as we skimmed through it together looking at different holistic offerings, including aromatherapy, nutrition seminars and other new approaches to wellness. One of the things Rose mentioned as she looked through the magazine with me was, "Even 'though I used to 'do' lots of 'New Age' stuff in college, I wouldn't have been comfortable trying any of these things at my stage of life if you hadn't shared with me some of the healing things you'd done yourself. You've mentioned certain holistic seminars and retreats you've gone to. By sharing that information, you gave me the confidence to pursue a more holistic repairing of my body."

I told Rose that I really appreciated her feedback. I felt validated in sharing more of my own experiences with clients than many therapists do. I also mentioned to her that I saw her efforts to reclaim her body becoming increasingly fine-tuned. "Finding specific interests like yoga or square dancing – going back to physical interests you had when younger is fine tuning. More than the walking, which you just began, you may find it easier to stick with some of the choices that come from your inner spirit!"

Rose responded, "Yes, I know what you mean because I don't always walk at lunch anymore. I don't really like walking but I think I'll enjoy yoga because I was successful with it before and I feel it's related to my spiritual yearnings."

Rose was beginning to reclaim her enthusiasm by surfacing positive memories from earlier in her life. So we see that as a client has increasing self-regard, she can find activities for herself that are reflections of her particular disposition and history. Of course, there's nothing wrong with walking, but it wasn't connected importantly to Rose's past. Yoga appeared to be a more precise fit. She had come up with this herself. My role was to support her expanded growth while helping her avoid regarding herself too harshly. I was excited by her progress, and shared my enthusiasm. Given her lost years, the broken feeling she had about herself and her obsessiveness, she was making great progress.

Sometimes a client needs to mirror the therapist, as Rose did my holistic interests. This is particularly useful with clients who suffer from diminished self-esteem and was a way to help Rose re-parent herself.

A week later Rose came in with a dream, "A wonderful dream," she told me. In it she was younger and thinner and walking across a large bridge. There was a little cubicle on the bridge where the gate-keeper sat. A storm came up. She remembered walking across the bridge in the rain and the wind. She could hardly keep her balance. At one point she was almost knocked unconscious. The handsome gatekeeper took her into his small apartment where he placed her on a bed in a very loving way. She dozed and eventually woke up. He made a move toward lovemaking in a most gentle, respectful and appropriate way. There was total mutual agreement.

Rose woke up from this dream feeling good. She went on to say that, of course, she felt some sadness because she didn't have a man in her life. I remarked that it was interesting that she was walking across a bridge and coming in from a terrible storm, as she is in a stage of her life where she is bridging from darkness to light. I also mentioned that I heard in the dream mutuality, comfort and sharing between herself and this man. Perhaps at the unconscious level this meant that she was moving past the brutality she felt with her husband and the resultant anger. This man treated her with respect and care. Rose liked the interpretation of the dream, saying, "I'm certainly not going to give up being me – it took me so long to get this far." We both laughed.

We can see the unconscious at work making efforts to restore Rose as a sexual being. My job was to validate her reemergence as a fully developed woman capable of a loving and sexual relationship regardless of whether she had yet begun to test the waters. I also tried to build her self-esteem by reminding her of the arduous journey she had been through successfully. Of course, this time that reminder was particularly meaningful because in her dream she had created the image of a storm.

Since that time Rose has continued to take small but significant steps: upgrading her job, and continuing to take care of her body. She does socialize more often, yet she has still not gone on that first date. Her mood is often lighter, she is less angry and there is less rumination.

Dana

Although a good high school student, Dana lived in a family where college was discouraged. Her expectations for herself were that she would marry early and work until she had a child. This is what happened. She married a young man whom she'd met in high school. Dana now forty-three, sought therapy because the marriage was in tatters, leaving her overwhelmed and very anxious. She mentioned frequent crying spells and feelings of despair. She thought separation was necessary, as her husband's verbal abuse and their frequent fighting were driving her away.

Early interviews in therapy revealed that Dana catered to her husband's needs, doing very little to develop herself in ways apart from her role as wife. At first I didn't understand clearly why she couldn't develop herself, but a clue appeared when she said, "My husband wouldn't give me the self-confidence to do things for myself" Apparently, Dana felt that self-confidence was a gift from her husband, one that he declined to offer, rather than a quality she owned.

In reviewing her life, we saw that as a child Dana had many interests, including music, sports and intellectual curiosity. But she had no support from family or community to pursue any of these interests. Her parents wanted her to be a "dutiful" daughter, who would marry young and establish a home nearby. Unfortunately, in school she was so retiring that teachers took little notice of her. As she grew up she was unaware of anyone who could be a mentor or supporter among her teachers or older children. Thus, as she so clearly and poignantly stated, she saw that her self-confidence would have to be given to her by her husband, the most significant figure in her world.

In the early stages of therapy I helped Dana get her bearings, work through some of her anger, and process more clearly some decisions regarding her marriage. Her husband refused to enter therapy with her or go on his own. She decided that divorce was necessary and that decision having been made, she and I worked on her own growth. I felt that I needed to stimulate her self-definition but that to do so, I would need to help her find some self-confidence within herself, not in another person. She had never taken a college course, never traveled, never gone into the nearby metropolis on her own. She left her home only to work in an office in her neighborhood. Yet Dana had many untapped interests: baseball, computers, art, cooking and eating fine foods. Whenever possible, I tried to reinforce the slightest moves she made toward any of these. By showing her true regard and interest in her efforts to reach out, I supported her developing self-esteem. In other words, I supplied the good-enough parenting she never received, that would have supported her growing into a more worldly and skilled and confident person.

As treatment continued, Dana moved to an apartment, leaving the neighborhood where she had grown up. She took a full-time job and met her women friends in the evenings to walk with them. Interest after interest began to emerge. I supported and encouraged her steps into the world, but she became her own navigator very quickly. As a matter of fact, her therapy was relatively brief. As her initial therapy terminated, Dana was ecstatic. She was taking her first major vacation in twenty years with her three women friends! They flew to Florida and then took a three day cruise during which she learned to scuba dive and fish. For Dana this was an amazing adventure. Her only regret was that she had not done something like this sooner.

Occasionally, Dana returns for several visits to process certain concerns. Last month she came in with some issues about her married daughter. She noted, "I really can't believe how I keep changing and growing. I'm having such a good time with my boyfriend. We hopped into the car and went on a little trip to Canada. It was a holiday weekend, and driving back we realized we would be late. And I just said to him, 'Let's not exhaust ourselves, let's stop in Boston and spend the day.' The next day we were having so much fun I called my job and said I'd be out an extra day. We were really living!"

I shared my delight with Dana. I said, "You seem so alive and you've grown so much! I remember when you took that first trip to Florida with your girlfriends. Now here you are in a significant relationship having fun, feeling at ease with your plans and really enjoying your life."

She added, "And what's even more amazing is that I can have a significant relationship and still really live. This is so different from my marriage. Last week my boyfriend and I were painting the front porch together and I made a mistake. We both just laughed and fixed it up. He didn't beat me up verbally, but in my marriage my husband and I could never do a project together without his putting me down. Now, I can be myself and make my own decisions and still have a significant relationship."

In therapy Dana needed and was given, a clear message early on that helped her validate what she probably already knew at the wise woman level – that no one should own another person's right to develop. Once I was able to help her see that her husband had violated her by constantly criticizing her and telling her, "You can't do that," she was quickly able to start the process of self-development. It was a process which ideally should have gone on twenty years earlier, but was now going on at record speed during her therapy. Understanding that she was responsible for her own self-worth and positive life choices, she quickly executed the development of latent talents and longings. Her ENCHANTED SELF began to emerge before I had even titled the concept. She retrieved for herself her studious side, her interest in travel, her interest in sports, her capacities to relate. Each was plucked like a blooming rose from the vine as she went into action. Currently, Dana has completed most of a junior college degree and has moved to a substantial full-time job.

In reviewing Dana's case, it's interesting to note that she neither exhibited any major characterlogical problems or other forms of severe pathology, but her apprehension over an impending marital breakup, her agitation and mild depression indicated that individual psychotherapy was the treatment of choice. However, I do wonder if Dana, or the many women, like her would need mental health care from a professional if our society encouraged them to develop self-esteem and a legitimate sense of identity for roles other than the traditionally "feminine" ones. Dana was certainly victimized by the narrow view of what a female could be-a view that she absorbed from her family, who absorbed it from the culture around them, without challenging these values. She then married a man with similar internalized notions who happened to be critical in nature and probably not very flexible. In twenty years this combination of factors resulted in a great deal of emotional stress. However, as soon as I was able to help her reframe her notions of the adult woman, i.e., her right to be self-confident and to develop her own identity, she was off like a tornado. In terms of clinical intervention she needed support, encouragement and a place to process after so many years of restricted living.

We need to remember that many of our clients may have mental health problems as a reaction to living situations. They themselves are not necessarily "ill." We must be careful never to make them feel as if they are ill.

In comparing Dana to Rose, there are significant clinical differences. Rose had characterlogical traits, particularly in the obsessive, compulsive area, that interfered with her execution of decisions. However, even in her treatment, these patterns did not become the primary focus. Once she was no longer frightened and overwhelmed by a cruel and oppressive relationship, she quickly educated herself about her obsessive-compulsive tendencies, and learned to modify them by attending many self-help groups. I believe it would have been less than fruitful and perhaps demoralizing for her, if I had focused my energies on those traits even though they were present. I chose, rather, to focus on the emerging sense of self.

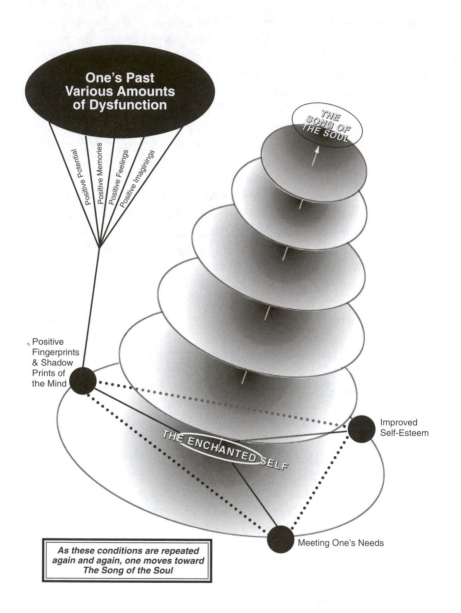

Before we go on, take a look at the diagram on page 94. You'll see at the bottom a gray space, suggesting the complexity of life's past experiences, out of which the therapist and/or yourself has hopefully begun to acknowledge good news about yourself or your client. Some of this good news represents positive memories, some positive imaginings, some wonderful feelings, aspirations or potential. They are now separated from the dark dysfunctional past where they could not be fully recognized, appreciated or properly labeled. Now you see them join in the circle which includes improved Self-Esteem, improved Need Satisfaction and the experience of ENCHANTED SELF states of being. The apex is the SONG OF THE SOUL. As a woman's self-esteem becomes a little stronger, as she learns to recognize unique talents and capacities, as she learns how to meet her needs and protect her personal space, then THE ENCHANTED SELF appears more often. Once it has emerged, the woman takes personal pleasure in recognizing her uniqueness and the expression of it, no matter how privately she does it. As personal space becomes better organized, needs are better organized and integrated. Healthier habits emerge such as more sleep or regular eating habits, seeking appropriate stimulation, singing in the car, working out, taking time for shopping or political activity. Whatever her needs, space and time dimensions are met a little more easily and continuously. Again, improvement releases more energies so that she finds herself able to tap into her Positive Fingerprints and Shadow Prints more often. We have this wonderful circular motion going on between improved self-esteem, improved personal boundaries and the emergence of ENCHANTED SELF material.

We see that without self-esteem, the circular loop which permits the emergence of THE ENCHANTED SELF cannot be achieved. Each of these two women was stymied until positive self-regard began to develop. In Dana's case, my reframing along with support was what was necessary. In Rose's case more was necessary, including self-help groups and working through a great deal of anger, along with support, encouragement, mirroring techniques and insight work. Dana was well on her way to singing Her SONG OF THE SOUL – she was alive and on target in many dimensions. Rose was still trying to experience and find Enchanted Moments. Yet each was on her way to utilizing positive aspects of herself in new adult ways.

Negative self-regard from internalized messages

A more complicated situation is where the client has many negative introjects. Rather than being sensitive and easily deflated by criticism from the outside (although this may also exist), she is her own worst critic. She carries internalized negative, self-defeating messages about herself. Here the therapist's task is more difficult than in the first two cases. This client requires your best training combined with a creative willingness to shift gears, making minor therapeutic alterations in style and technique, to help break down the internalized barriers. You and she are fighting against a tyrant. This tyrant is the deeply entrenched super ego, ferociously monitoring any efforts you and she might make to change the status quo. Nonetheless, enhancing growth is still possible. This vigilant part of us that watches our behaviors is normal and developmentally appropriate if it can develop some flexibility as we grow older. For some people, particularly those who experience many negative criticisms in early childhood, the super ego becomes rigidly entrenched and sees behaviors as either black or white. Often, people who have experienced negative criticism in childhood find it hard to compromise either with themselves or with others. Sometimes they are harder on themselves than on anyone else.

Dorothy

Dorothy entered psychotherapy in her mid-forties, struggling with depressive feelings as well as with agitation. She talked about coming from a professional home where both parents were physics professors at a famous men's college. Her father was from France and very authoritarian in his attitudes. She was well aware of early messages she'd absorbed. As she put it, "It was clearly wrong to be the kind of attractive girl who might be construed as provocative or forward in any way. A girl should be kind, nurturing, industrious, hard working, domestic, chaste and good. Additionally, she should be intelligent and engaged in scholarly pursuits as an end or as a pleasure for their own sake." Dating was discouraged but, "Somewhere, sometime one magically became an adult and Prince Charming would magically appear on the horizon if – and only if – one followed certain rules and molded oneself a certain way."

Once she had met the potential partner, the only questions she could ask herself were, "Did he find me suitable, in other words, pretty, modest, helpful, cooperative, etc.?" As Dorothy said, there was never any sense of mutuality in building a relationship. The job of adapting would always remain hers.

In childhood Dorothy was forced to monitor her behavior very strictly, according to her parents' rules. She could not make noise or openly play. One of the only things she was allowed to do was to sit on the couch and read. For most of her childhood, she felt as though she was without power. Children were to be seen but not heard. Dorothy became such an avid reader that she often read more than one book a day. She remembers feeling good as she sat alone reading but also remembers that there was no choice of activity. However, it did provide privacy and a time and a place for enchantment. Dorothy remembers going back and forth to the library as a minor autonomous act that felt good because it was one of the only few autonomous acts she was permitted. When Dorothy was in trouble with her parents, she was often slapped across the face and sent to her room. Many times she missed meals for minor transgressions. She often felt powerless to control the rage that might be thrown at her by one or both parents.

Needless to say, aside from going to college, Dorothy yearned to find her Prince Charming so that she could move from her household. She stated, "I was the classic Sleeping Beauty, waiting for it all to happen — waiting for the person, the kiss, the opportunity and for life to present itself to me. I felt I would come alive when I was loved or in a supportive relationship. I could love myself when someone else loved me, but not necessarily otherwise. If I wasn't loved, my unlovableness and unacceptability were confirmed."

Dorothy couldn't develop positive self-regard, and believed she could find it only through the love of another. Dorothy was an eager psychotherapy client. She often told me that this was her chance, perhaps her only chance, to really talk about herself and find a way to get out of some of the frustrating circles of behavior in which she found herself. She did marry and had two daughters, teenagers when she entered therapy. She loved her husband but found that their relationship contained much unresolved anger. Their interests were different and they were both busy with frantic professional activities as

97

well as with all the activities and transporting of their teenage daughters. There was seldom serenity in the house. Dorothy wished that she and her husband could talk to each other rather than fight. She saw herself attempting to keep the peace by denying her own feelings. She often sputtered in rage and anger and had poor negotiating skills. Of course I suggested many times that Dorothy invite her husband to participate in couple's therapy or that he seek individual therapy. She reported that he saw therapy as frivolous and would never try it. I encouraged her, nonetheless, to inform him what we talked about, if she wanted to, and to leave the door open for him to join her occasionally. She agreed to do that.

Early in the treatment, we worked intensely on the development of negotiating skills within the marriage as well as within the family. Teaching Dorothy certain skills was technically easy in the sense that she was brilliant, but many internalized negative messages got in the way. She saw herself as a non-agent, dependent on her husband taking the lead.

When we could work our way through one roadblock, we would discover another – such as an internalized belief system that harbored the notions that relationships had no permanence and that good things did not happen in relationships, or that good things would not last. These internalized storylines made Dorothy so cautious and hesitant that it was almost impossible for her to mobilize and take any risks within her various relationships.

Dorothy had also isolated herself by exercising little power in her relationships. As the treatment went on, I wanted to help her develop some sense of self-regard that would really begin to work for her. Although she seemed to take pleasure from the detailed storytelling of her life to me, she did not respond well to my feedback. No matter how supportive I tried to make my reactions, I seemed to make her feel as if I'd taken a sledge hammer and wounded her. She might begin to cry or come in very quiet the next time. Then we might have a session of virtual silence. It became apparent when she did open up that often a word I had used had been misinterpreted or a concept I was trying to explain had been exaggerated and taken personally.

Without taking the reader through a long process of psychotherapy of several years duration, I want to describe the moment when we were able to finally create an effective working alliance. Dorothy had told me many times and in many ways how critically sensitive she was to any one in an authoritarian position. Her parents, as brilliant professors, had hundreds of times demoralized her. She respected me and saw me as possessing a type of knowledge that she did not. One day, she came in carrying a book written by a psychiatrist. She mentioned a case study in the book where instead of asking the client to lie down on the couch, the therapist changed the positioning so that they were face-to-face. Of course in her therapy, we were already face-to-face but I was clearly in an authoritarian position in the therapist's chair. I asked her what she found so intriguing about this book and Dorothy responded that she thought it was something to do with the reciprocal nature the psychiatrist was able to establish with his client rather than one-up, one-down. I asked her if she wanted more of that with me. She said, "I do, because I can see I keep lapsing into a one-down position – taking everything you say in an exaggerated way. Then I just leave emotionally, I close up and go to some vacant, protective space. I asked how she thought we might be able to do that and she said, "Well, maybe if you sit on the couch and I sit on the couch." We discussed this and decided that starting with the next session, we would both sit on the couch. This new seating arrangement continued for many months. Dorothy explained that sitting across from me and seeing me as the authoritarian figure just furthered the distance between the listener and the speaker, which she found incredibly painful. Because so much of her psychological pain was around isolation, feeling disconnected in the therapy hour intensified her pain. Since we began the new seating arrangement, Dorothy has never broken into profound tears or isolated herself during the therapy session. She talked about how she was forced to be the invisible child and how, when she's put on the spot, she feels as if she's being watched and this "kills something" inside of her. In our new seating arrangement she doesn't feel that way. She feels a true reciprocity.

In one session Dorothy talked about spending time with her friend, a chemist. She'd often bemoaned the fact that she did not become a chemist herself. I reminded her of many of her own talents, which include a love of pharmacology, similar to her great grandfather's. I also reiterated my appreciation for information she shared

99

with me about medications. I mentioned that even though she might not have been able to find a way to utilize this passion as a career, I saw her knowledge of pharmacology as a vital, special part of her. It was part of her identity and added something to many people's lives. I reminded her that the information she gave me about a medication my father was taking had been very helpful to the family.

Rather than becoming downcast or withdrawn as she might have done in the past, Dorothy smiled and remained able to relate, actually shifting the subject to say that she was attempting to process the notions of THE ENCHANTED SELF that I had shared with her previously. What had frustrated her about the concept, she said, was that she felt she had so little positive information to retrieve from her own past. The only good moments were spent in her imagination, reading novels. We talked about this capacity and I reinforced for her my sense that retrieving positive moments from one's imagination was just as legitimate as retrieving positive information from an actualized past event. She laughed and said, "That's good. I've got a lot of imagination to work with!"

This case is important because it illustrates how internalized barriers kept Dorothy from the very growth that she yearned for and how they were dissolved in therapy. Exquisitely sensitive to others, as well as having internalized little positive self-regard, she couldn't flower at all except in a reciprocal relationship. When she felt inferior she easily distorted and exaggerated my interventions, further augmenting inferiority and guilt feelings. But when she felt like an equal to me she was able to hear me more accurately. My technique didn't really change. I still behaved as a therapist but by listening to her request and moving to the other end of the couch I made it possible for her to feel that we were working partners. As I write, positive self-regard is just developing in Dorothy and she's starting to work on her ENCHANTED SELF. For example, rather than closing down in the therapy hour as she once did, she actually led the discussion back to a concept she wished to pursue – leading her to explain further her negative childhood memories. This gave me a chance to reframe for her the concept of positive memories to include those imagined rather than only those that happened. Dorothy now joined in the pursuit of positive memories of her imagination. Soon, when she distorts our communication even less, I expect that she'll start the circular movement between retrieval of positive imaginings, recovered positive real happenings, and some emerging self-regard. I anticipate her understanding how the family's dysfunction interfered with her development. I look forward to the time when she can reclaim her talents, capacities and potential, no longer burdened by the damage of the early dysfunction that led to distorted internalized self-messages. Finally, we'll work on better ways for her to get her needs met as she becomes less frightened of negotiating in her significant relationships.

The results of positive self-regard

Stacy

As we conclude this chapter, Stacy comes to mind. As Stacy began to work on positive self-regard, she became more comfortable in her marriage. She was also better able to negotiate. And not least, she began to experience more joy.

Stacy entered therapy feeling anxious and depressed after the early death of her older brother whom she had nursed intensively for many years. Preoccupation with his illness had kept her from making many of the normal decisions that young women make in their twenties and thirties. Any leftover energy went to parent her teenage daughter and in working part time. Her husband, preoccupied with his career, was often quite critical.

A goal of Stacy's therapy was to help her define her own sense of worth, now that her brother had died. She had to take back her own life. Aside from lost time she, like Dana, did not have serious pathology. She was unsure of herself in many social and personal situations. Literally, her head had been in the sickroom for fifteen years.

We worked first on techniques of getting her appropriate needs met as well as orchestrating the needs of her family. She learned quickly. Stacy, unlike Dorothy, had not absorbed extremely negative messages about herself. She'd simply given herself over to a family situation that went on and on. Now she had to practice taking herself back. Toward the end of her therapy, she came in with some good news – news that I considered significant because it suggested that she that had reowned herself, learned how to negotiate and was being truer to her own ENCHANTED SELF.

She'd gone with her husband and teenage daughter to look at a small sailboat to purchase. The boat appeared to Stacy not to be as seaworthy as her husband and daughter assumed. Although she knew little about sailboats, her instincts told her they should not make an immediate purchase. Her husband and daughter were eager to sign on the spot and pick up the boat the next day. Stacy suggested quietly to her husband that they think this over and postpone signing the contract. Because of Stacy's quiet and sensitive manner as she spoke, her husband relinquished control and they left without purchasing the boat. However, as soon as they were in the car he started yelling at her, saying "Why didn't you let me buy the boat – it was perfect for us – what's going on here?" Stacy merely said she wanted to do some more research and felt that it didn't seem quite right to make that hasty a deal. Her daughter complained, "Mom, how could you not let us buy it?" However, Stacy held firm and made some telephone calls. The calls confirmed her intuition. If it were damaged, she learned, the boat would cost so much to fix that it would be much smarter to buy a more expensive boat in the first place. Stacy shared her findings without anger with her husband, and he agreed not to purchase the boat. Several days later, a more suitable boat was found and purchased.

Within twelve hours, another significant event occurred. Stacy's creative urge led her to stay up late that night. She set up her sewing machine in the kitchen and started to make a small quilt. She made herself a cup of tea, put the radio on to her favorite music and worked into the night finishing half of the quilt. She liked what she had done and hung it on the wall over the kitchen table. The next morning when her husband came down, he saw the quilt hanging on the wall and Stacy waited for his reaction. He thought for a while and finally said, "Well, that certainly looks like you did it." That was all the praise he was able to muster! However, this didn't deter Stacy from finishing the quilt and hanging it carefully on a special matting. She was proud of it. I applauded Stacy for having been able to move forward in her own growth in two basic dimensions. First she was able to hold onto a very strong sense of self-regard and self-worth even though she'd received negative feedback from her family about the boat. She was even able to utilize her instincts that are so often correct. Often we have intuitive knowledge that something is best done or left undone, but when we are beaten up for not having the proper facts, statistics or knowledge, we cave in or end up believing that we were indeed wrong in our opinions. I shared all of this with Stacy and congratulated her on being able to sustain the negative feedback, validate her position and make the facts clear to her family all within twelve hours, without any display of anger. She'd shown tremendous stamina and the ability to take a clear position.

Her second adventure late at night displayed how she was freeing her own creative energies. This seemed to be coming from a place deep inside her that went back to an early love of sewing and color that she had often talked about. Her husband was certainly not about to compliment her. To be told that something looks like your own production, seemed to me neither a compliment nor an insult. However, I explained to Stacy that many people might perceive his remark as an insult. What was so wonderful in her case was that she was able to accept his feedback as simply his type of feedback and basically disregard it. She could go ahead with her project, seeing its full value and proudly hanging it in her own home where it deserved to be hung. She had become her own best critic!

Her therapy hour was a congratulatory session where I was able to praise Stacy for her two major successes. The hard work had already taken place and now she was reaping the rewards of a person freed to become a fully adult person.

Conclusion

This concludes the chapter on how positive self-esteem can be stimulated by the therapist and how it interweaves itself into the process of getting in touch with THE ENCHANTED SELF. By sharing some of my own self-esteem issues as well as my clients', I've given a sense of how profoundly important positive self-regard is in reaching a joyful integrative adult state. I've placed the external values of our culture in some perspective, and described the delicate balance that exists between positive self-regard, meeting one's needs, and an awareness of the individual's capacities for joy. Internalizing a sense of self-worth and positive self-regard that is not dependent on external cues is no small task. All of us, including clinicians, may struggle with it but it's well worth the struggle! As we come closer to experiencing positive self-regard, we come closer to enhanced joyful living, and experiencing our ENCHANTED SELVES.

Readers' exercise

1. Please write down five positive comments about yourself. For example, "You are a most courteous and helpful person." "You are always there for me." "I can always trust you." You can make these statements in the first person or the third person, whichever is more comfortable for you. For example, you could state, "I'm a courageous person who tries to help others out even at great cost to myself." Or you could say, "You are a most courageous person who is willing to help others out, even at great cost to yourself."

After you have made your list of five positive remarks you'd like to hear about yourself, put this piece of paper in your wallet or pocket-book. Read it to yourself at least once a day for one week. You may think of other positive statements you'd like to add, or you may get tired of certain ones and delete them. That's fine, just keep the number around five.

2. After a week, answer the following questions:

(a) How did you feel reading these remarks?

(b) Were there remarks you wished you could have made but honestly felt you didn't deserve? If so, what do you think are some of the things you might need to work on before you can legitimately make a particular statement? Jot down some of those things. Try to be objective. Is your list realistic? Too perfectionistic? If it is perfectionistic, try to make it more realistic. Remember that incorporating positive self-regard requires practice and repetition just as incorporating negative self-statements required repetition. If you find this exercise uncomfortable at this time, return to it later.

3. Make a SELF PRIDE list. For those of you who may find it difficult to enumerate clearly some of your positive capacities, I suggest that you keep a journal for a week. During the week, write down at least one item a day that you can take pride in having handled well. For example, on your list you might find, "I was polite and kind to several people in the check out line in the supermarket, even though I was tired." Or you might write another comment such as, "I used my head rather than my fist and really shared with

my son my concerns over his getting another traffic ticket, rather than showing intense anger." Or you might write something as simple as, "I took care of my body today. I ate reasonable foods and went for a walk."

At the end of the week, read over your list three times at one sitting. After you've done that, give yourself a mental hug or visualize yourself shaking your hand or giving yourself the "high five" sign, or even placing a gold star on your forehead. Give yourself some recognition!

Chapter Nine

Meeting Our Needs

I N each of these chapters we're learning how to live a maximally enhanced life and experiencing positive states of being, unique to each of us, which I call THE ENCHANTED SELF.

As noted, the best place, by far, to find the enhanced self is in our past – no matter how many minefields lurk there. No matter how disappointing childhood, or the more recent past, has been, the past weaves the fabric and contains the memory bank from which everyone's character has been molded. For each of us, it is from that reservoir of life's experiences that we create a sense of identity and personal history. Therefore, it is extremely important to retrieve from our pasts workable positive memories, even if they must be sifted and separated from gravel and dirt. We must look for golden nuggets, be they events, feelings or positive imaginings. No individual can be as close or as intimate to another as you are to your own self. The curative effect of finding one's own golden nuggets is profound because it is immediate and personal rather than vicarious (as from a book or movie).

We don't just live in the present – each of us contains a system of memories and feelings, needs and desires, ideas and notions, philosophies and ego states. We are the only beings truly able to contain and live with the priceless configuration that comprises our identity. This is where THE ENCHANTED SELF as a technique parts company with other humanistic psychologies that give more generalized instructions or guidelines for recovery.

Let me explain: In most humanistic seminars, workshops or materials, suggested techniques often focus on relaxation methods, directed visualizations, designs for change, or problem-solving strategies that may not take the individual's personal history into account. They are present-centered, not individually tailored to each participant's history, needs and/or agenda. Perhaps that's why so often people leave such seminars or workshops high and inspired, only to crash emotionally back into old habits weeks or months later.

THE ENCHANTED SELF also differs from standard dynamic psychotherapies that focus on the past, often on the pain that has been experienced in the past or on the wounded child who survives the past, rather than on the retrieval of positive memories. Although, like all psychotherapies, the goal of dynamic psychotherapies is to change and illuminate behavior, they often emphasize dysfunctional pain to be "worked through" rather than accessing the positive hopes, dreams and behaviors that were also once present. Overlooking or minimizing the positive can result in a tremendous loss of the potential psychic energy that resides in all of us. Even if we are profoundly wounded, even if we keep making the same mistakes, we all yearn for the fullest possible restoration of the self.

In Chapters VI and VII, I discussed helping clients and ourselves access positive memories, both realized and imagined from our own past, i.e., Positive Fingerprints of the Mind, and Positive Shadow Prints of the Mind. This task involved certain tools that one could bring into the therapy or that one could use personally, including renaming, reframing, and the separation of dysfunctional aspects of one's past from the functional.

In Chapter VIII, I discussed how achieving self-esteem facilitates the emergence of THE ENCHANTED SELF. If one doesn't regard the self positively, then one won't have the emotional energy necessary to look within and develop enhanced capacities and talents. The energy will not be there to free the self from negative labels that result from a dysfunctional childhood or from recent negative experiences, so we cannot sing THE SONG OF THE SOUL.

In this Chapter, I discuss the importance of helping our clients to get needs met. No matter how accurately one may recognize her own talents and potential, no matter how energetically she works for the retrieval of positive memories and no matter how much self-esteem she develops as she gains this positive knowledge of herself, she cannot actualize positive states of being, i.e., THE ENCHANTED SELF, unless her needs are met

Remember: THE ENCHANTED SELF technique is designed to teach you to orient yourself and your clients to positive rather than negative aspects of the self, learning how to recognize and encourage THE ENCHANTED SELF, i.e., positive states of being that incorporate traces of one's uniqueness.

A major source of dysfunction is not being able to get needs met. There are several reasons why clients may have trouble with this

1. They are unaware of their needs.
2. Their intimates are unable (crazy, unintelligent, immature, unwilling, cruel, dismissive, or stubborn) to meet their needs.
3. They can't or won't express their needs – too timid, withdrawn, frightened, don't have the language, or don't think they deserve need satisfaction.

Most psychotherapy helps people with all of the above except where a client is in a job or intimate situation where someone else is unwilling or unable to meet their needs. The therapist can, however still help the client recognize the futility of getting her needs met in such a case and then facilitate development so the person can move out of the situation and into one that's more promising.

How ENCHANTED SELF therapy helps when need-satisfaction is blocked

1. WHEN CLIENTS ARE UNAWARE OF THEIR NEEDS.
Because ENCHANTED SELF therapy encourages constant sorting through states of mind, searching for and learning to recognize positive states of being, the process lends itself to clarification of one's needs. Often psychotherapeutic techniques emphasize the search for dysfunction, highlighting what has made the person feel

uncomfortable or pained. We don't spend much time helping the person discover what feels exactly right. If we don't know how it feels when we are centered, on the right track, "in tune," then we can't design the techniques to get there. THE ENCHANTED SELF technique, because it applauds and documents what is most life-enhancing about each of us, makes clearer where we should aim. Once the target is established, traditional psychotherapeutic approaches can be utilized to help the person get there.

2. WHEN THE CLIENT'S INTIMATES ARE UNABLE TO MEET THEIR NEEDS. People often face situations where others in their lives are unwilling or unable to meet their needs. ENCHANTED SELF therapy helps in these cases by directing clients to look for their strengths and potential as well as by encouraging self-esteem. As clients develop the above self-perceptions they are stronger and better able to recognize inadequacies in other people and situations rather than assuming that they are at fault. People enter psychotherapy in such a vulnerable state and so worn down, that much of the time is spent trying to help them see that they're not solely responsible for a particular difficulty. Often this insight comes late in therapy. There's much more chance that it will come earlier when therapy emphasizes strengths rather than weaknesses. In other words, if I can say: "I feel entitled to be treated well, I'll be more open to learning how to ask for good treatment from others than if I feel I am not deserving." If the significant others will not meet the client halfway, then her new self-esteem is invaluable in helping her to move along to other friends or contexts where she is more likely to find cooperation.

3. WHEN PEOPLE CAN'T OR WON'T EXPRESS THEIR NEEDS. ENCHANTED SELF therapy helps when people can't or won't express their needs, by providing an environment where there is more leverage and more energy, so that the client is willing to work on learning how to get needs met. It is what I call a "holding environment" (described below) between client and therapist, that has certain unique features that heighten the learning.

The holding environment

As the therapist, you must be willing and available to confirm, acknowledge and often teach the client that meeting her own needs requires giving oneself permission to self-replenish. No matter how your client perceives herself, whether as giver, as taker, or perhaps as a perfectionist or a controller, and regardless of what she is working on, she still needs to replenish herself. Many clients do not feel entitled to this. They see themselves as "givers" and feel that they will become "takers" if they ask for nurturing, or loving, help or time from someone else. The therapist may need to teach the client about reciprocal relationships where one gives as well as takes Positive taking does not drain the other. It's usually refreshing for the giver also.

It's also within the holding environment that the therapist teaches the client that she has permission to honor a sacred place within herself – a private space that is not necessarily open to others. We have the right to design and cultivate our lives according to our needs in the physical, emotional, social and cognitive spheres. No one has the right to intrude if such intrusion results in violation or depletion. This private, often sacred space, is highly individual and unique. We do not need awards, competition, success or fame to enter this space. By helping your client find this treasure and teaching her how to protect her sacredness, you lead her not only to better mental health and more enhanced living, but you contribute to a more respectful society.

ENCHANTED SELF technique utilized in helping people access their needs

1. Utilize the retrieval of POSITIVE FINGERPRINTS of the MIND and POSITIVE SHADOWS of the MIND to teach your client how to discriminate and recognize legitimate earlier needs. This teaching can happen naturally as you sift through her dysfunctional past to find the happy times. As you discuss the dysfunctional aspects of prior life situations, you can easily point out where her needs were not met. For example, if a client loved paper dolls but her mother consistently threw her creations away while cleaning up, one could discuss the positive feelings, strengths and talent that existed as she made the paper dolls, while still processing how her mother's intrusion, disrespect and control may all have interfered with her

111

freedom to execute an early love. The goal is to help the client retrieve and reintegrate aspects of these earlier positive states of being into current positive states of being. The client can identify and appreciate her legitimate childhood needs. Therapy also can assist her in developing new ways to satisfy similar or identical needs.

2. Encourage your clients to return to positive rather than negative ego states. As noted before, clients may feel that it's natural and appropriate to return to paralyzing negative states of being because the return to the painful past has been so often emphasized in many psychotherapies.

THE ENCHANTED SELF technique provides you with a wonderful instrument to help your clients, through teaching and positive reinforcement, to develop the habits necessary to return to positive states of being. You can help her to recognize, value and feel entitled to positive states of mind. You can facilitate the psychological learning necessary to successfully integrate these states of well-being into their present lives. Visual imagery, art, journal-writing, role-playing, cognitive and behavioral techniques can all be utilized to practice patterns of positive behavior.

For instance, I ask clients to document how well they're doing. Example: a client was being put down by her boss who was trying to convince her that she was an inadequate employee. As the client noted, "She wanted me to believe her storyline about myself." The client went on to say that each morning as she drove to work, she listed all the positive things she had been able to do thus far that day. "I made breakfast for the family, I fed the dog and walked her, I started some laundry, I set up meal preparations for tonight, I balanced my checkbook, I looked at the newspaper and I called my mother and checked on her health. If I were as inadequate as this women wants me to think I am, I couldn't possibly have done what I did in 45 minutes." The client then went on to mention that before her therapy she would not have been able to enumerate so many positive aspects of herself, particularly when she was on her way to confront a person who was trying to make her feel impaired. This client was learning how to keep affirmations like these, so when pressured by a negative manager she was able to automatically go back to her own reinforcing statements rather than to old patterns of thinking that included damaging put downs.

3. Emphasize a client's strengths rather than weaknesses. In utilizing THE ENCHANTED SELF therapy, a clinician can teach the good news that as we let go of traits that are not working in our best interests, we free ourselves to better experience the breadth and depth of life. As the therapist emphasizes these strengths and as the person feels herself stronger, she is more willing to relinquish negative patterns of behavior. As mentioned in Chapter VII, directly pointing out pathology too often results in destructive negative thinking that your client can turn against herself or which can interfere with trust in the therapeutic relationship. By concentrating on the person's strengths, the therapist can take the lead from her client and let the client determine what should be modified and how. People get satisfaction by developing their strengths. Of course, there may be at least some pathology there, too. The clinician must be wise enough to know how to point out the strengths that may reside within the pathology without breaking the client's spirit. Let me show you what I mean by describing Tom.

Tom, a caring, concerned person, could be a bully when trying to make his point. Not only did he bully his wife, he also blasted his children. I pointed out the destructive aspects of the bully side of his nature, but I spent most of my teaching time emphasizing the strengths latent in his "bully" persona. How much force could be freed, how capable he could be in pleading on his own or another's behalf, if he could use his tremendous energy and his strong convictions constructively and not explosively.

I also taught him how others feel when they are bossed around, without clear regard to their preferences, capacities or feelings. By accessing and utilizing a talent rather than trying to get rid of a liability, Tom could accomplish a lot. Because I also worked with him and his wife, Helen, in couple's therapy, I was able to point out, with her help, the destructive side of his bossiness while still emphasizing his potential. This was greatly assisted by his wife's comments and feedback. She could tell him how she felt when he really listened to the family and reacted with regard, taking his time to modulate his responses. Tom profited from the "good news" about his strengths. He was also able to understand how his behavior affected his relationships. He began to use better judgment although he always maintained a somewhat bombastic style, particularly when threatened. He was able to turn his tendency to be forceful and controlling into a skill for politics. At last report he was running for a county office, and enjoying every moment of the election process as well as hoping to make some positive changes at the county level.

Thus, ENCHANTED SELF therapy provides both a holding and a teaching environment that is useful in helping people meet their own needs. Let's look at a few more cases that illustrate the above principles in ENCHANTED SELF Therapy.

Julia

Julia, a beautiful woman in her late forties, dresses elegantly and carries herself proudly. A successful businesswoman, Julia commutes between New York and Philadelphia for her investment business. Married for twenty-eight years, she came into therapy distressed by overwhelming fatigue and anxiety as well as with some mild depression that she frequently experienced after being with her husband or her father. Julia's mother died several years before she entered therapy, leaving her father increasingly dependent, making demands that, to Julia, seemed unnecessary. Her early sessions focused on teaching her more successful ways of negotiating her own needs with her father. This included teaching her how to express herself to him without becoming agitated, either externally or internally, and how to listen more accurately and empathetically to him so that she could strategically plan for his real needs to be met. After these sessions Julia felt empowered because she had successfully, yet in a caring fashion, safeguarded her space. Fortunately she'd been able to help him move to an appropriate retirement setting and he now had friends and other relatives nearby.

At this point in therapy, we shifted to her relationship with her husband. Julia felt that her husband violated her in many ways: he interrupted her; he would wake her if she had just drifted off; he publicly disqualified and belittled what she said in conversation with others. He claimed to love her dearly and, to her knowledge, he was faithful to her. However, his behaviors were wearing her out. She was furious at him. At times he ripped her heart out and then she would feel miserable, as if she were nothing.

In one session, she discussed a recent conversation with her husband. He'd been going over their personal finances and said,

114

"We've had a very good year, Julia. If you want to go to that health spa that you like so much in Florida, I think we can afford it." Then he added, "It will help you look better."

This remark cut Julia like a knife. She gathered her strength and said, "What do you mean?" He said, "Well you know you could look better." Julia started to cry and she also cried with me. "He's done this to me so many times. Even when I was young and beautiful, he always made me feel fat and ugly. I always worried that I looked foolish in a bathing suit. Now I'm turning fifty! I feel good physically; I'm making a lot a money and I want to live in harmony with myself and with life. I don't want to be emotionally drained every time I talk to my husband.

"These feelings go back to childhood. My dad would walk into the room and say, 'Julia, isn't that dress wrinkled? Why don't you try to take a little bit better care of yourself.' And I would be crushed. I remember a night out with my husband when we were in our twenties. We went to an expensive restaurant and my mouth was watering. I ordered a lobster smothered in butter and when the woman taking the order asked if I would like a baked potato with it, my husband said, "No, she'll skip the baked potato." He turned to me and said something like, 'Julia, when will you finally take off some weight?' I was not even heavy – maybe I'd gained a few extra pounds from having a baby the year before. I felt miserable after his comment and by the time the lobster came I couldn't even enjoy it – I only ate two or three bites. And do you know what that rat did? He ate the lobster on top of his own steak! He should have choked!"

I listened to Julia's story, offering nods and concerned looks. Then I said to her, "I can feel your pain, myself. How sad that your husband was so insensitive as to offer the spa, something that you would have enjoyed doing, in the way of an insult! Also, I can see how sensitive you would be in issues concerning your body and appearance since your father also zeroed in on how you looked. I know just what you mean about an energy drain. There are times when people make us feel weak and powerless. Perhaps there are some techniques you could learn that would keep your husband more in line. Certainly not enjoying your lobster years ago and watching him eat it, or crying about it now don't seem to be adequate solutions for negotiating with your husband. Since he is not in therapy and is disinterested in joining us, I can't guarantee that we can change him. However, I think it's important to take a clearer stand with him and let him know when he is out of bounds. Sometimes it helps to use feeling statements such as, 'What you just said makes me feel bad. I don't know if you meant to insult me, but that's the way I felt when I heard you talk about me going to the spa. You made me feel as though you see me as someone who's not physically pleasing to you. I feel good about my looks and I would only go to the spa for replenishment.' Perhaps a remark such as that would make him back up and reframe what he was trying to say or reframe in your best interests, even if he had less caring thoughts on his mind. It's important that he know how you feel about yourself."

I also suggested we talk further about the significance to her of her longtime marriage to her.

During future sessions we discussed her needs as they related to her partnership. She was able to clearly identify a need to stay in the marriage based on love for him, the world they shared and as a correction for the lack of family warmth she had experienced while growing up. When not angry they were very affectionate and loving. They met at many levels: as best friends, as compatible lovers, as parents of loved children. Yet she began to realize that her need to be treated decently outweighed everything else. If she could not negotiate better with him so that he would change toward her in areas that were very important to her, she was determined to leave.

Over the next several months, I continued to teach Julia various coping strategies. She learned enthusiastically and quickly. At the same time she fought the intrusion of old feelings whenever her husband violated her. Thus her reactions were sometimes intensified. During these months, I pursued more in-depth psychotherapy around early traumas utilizing standard insight methods, so that each time these feelings were triggered, they were less disturbing.

Several months later Julia came in as gorgeous as ever, this time truly glowing. "I've gotten there, I'm finally at a place where I can walk away, if I have to. No one, including my husband, can take my self-esteem away from me anymore. I'll tell you what happened. We were at our weekend home. I was watching a show on television and he insisted on talking on the phone just to bother me. When I asked him to use the phone in the other room, he became verbally abusive.

Later, he came back in and said, 'Don't you ever make me go in the other room like that,' and then he swore, slammed the door to the den and locked it. At first, I went into the bedroom and had a good cry. I know this wasn't the most effective response but I had to cry or I couldn't have gone on. Then I pulled myself together and said to myself, 'I'm hungry,' and I took the car and went out and had a lovely dinner. When I got home, he was still in the den and I went to sleep.

"The next day happened to be my birthday and lo and behold he gave me some very beautiful cards, flowers and a lovely scarf. I accepted them all very nicely, but then I said to him in a quiet clear voice, 'If you ever talk to me again the way you did last night, if you use that tone of voice and make negative remarks, I guarantee you that I'll get in the car and go back to New Jersey. You won't even know I'm gone until you come to the bedroom to look for me or take the car keys and look for the car. I will not communicate with you and you'll be stranded. If you have an issue with me, I'm willing to discuss it, but if you abuse me, I will not tolerate being abused.'" Her husband responded merely by saying, "Okay."

This was one of Julia's good news reports before she terminated therapy. Julia's husband was a man who exhibited a great deal of dys–functional behavior. He was a bully in style but appeared deeply committed to the marriage, as was Julia, although, as I noted above, he would not join us in therapy. Therefore Julia had to develop ways of getting his attention, so that he realized that she would really insist on the inviolability of her feelings and some reasonable space for herself while they still remained a viable couple. Coming on strong, loud and clear worked – not crying and certainly not just taking it.

At her last session, Julia said, "I finally feel in harmony with myself. I have a wonderful, loving relationship with my daughter. We're best friends and we have lots of fun and laughter together. I'm enjoying every moment with her baby, too. It's pure joy. There's a feeling of connection between the three of us that I can't begin to put into words. It's the womanly experience of sharing generations that's free from the hassle of bitter words. It's like the best times in my childhood when I hung out at grandma's – the cousins and aunts in the kitchen – the smells!

"And also, now, I have my own special private times that no one else knows about, like listening to New Age music in the car, long

117

walks on the beach and just being there for myself in a way that no one can get to me.

"And now I've got the power to assert myself in my marriage ... a sense of identity and of being a whole person. If I need to go it alone, I'll be fine. If not, at least I'm a real person in my marriage."

Julia succeeded in upgrading her coping skills so that she was able to meet her personal needs and develop improved self-esteem particularly in relation to her husband. Not feeling as much violation by him, she was also making progress in creating her own quality time. Although she might not achieve consistent gratification with her husband, she was determined to stay with him for many valid reasons. Yet she and he both knew that if pushed beyond her limits of personal dignity and integrity, she would leave. By improving her communications skills their relationship changed. She now had more energy for her own private times as well as time with other people – times when she was able to feel true joy.

Stephanie

Stephanie is a bright, articulate and professionally successful middle-aged woman, capable of raucous humor. She has a fierce tongue and holds nothing back. Growing up in a house dominated by a harsh grandmother, she developed, she says, a wise self-knowledge when she was only a tiny child. This wisdom gave her a feeling of control (although she could never exercise this as a child) and a secret sense of being in possession of the truth. She was aware, even as a young-ster, of how psychologically inept her grandmother was, relying on forcefeeding Stephanie and choosing her clothing for her even as she grew old enough to do so herself. Grandmother also did not permit her much, privacy, not even in the bathroom.

Wise, but unable to effectuate any real control of her grand-mother, Stephanie developed many controlling mechanisms as an adult, such as bossiness and criticality. She scrutinized the expendi-tures made by her first husband and even dictated the temperature of their house. From a previous therapy she developed insight into her need to dominate and control relationships.

Stephanie had gotten divorced many years ago and had a married son. She reentered therapy because of acute anxiety regarding her new marriage. She was well aware of her tendency to control rather than to process a relationship. Tragically, before we could work through her emotional issues, she discovered a lump in her breast, that along with several swollen lymph nodes turned out to be malignant. She was fighting for her life. After a mastectomy Stephanie began the arduous treatments of chemotherapy and radiation.

One day she came in particularly distressed, telling me that she was withdrawing from all of those who cared dearly for her, especially from one friend who constantly gave her information about cancer research – information that overwhelmed her. She also pulled back from another friend who always asked her how she was feeling and what was happening in her treatment. She also withdrew from her husband because he would sit around the house looking morose and preoccupied when she wanted to forget her medical problems and just go on living with him as a couple.

Stephanie adored her husband. They shared many hobbies and interests that they had just begun to develop and make a part of their marriage. She mentioned that isolating was an old "trick" of hers that she used again and again when her grandmother became too intrusive and dominating. She could go days without saying anything and even became expert at keeping her mouth clenched when her grandmother tried to forcefeed her.

We talked about Stephanie's withdrawal as an old defense. It made perfect sense that she would go back to that pattern of behavior. However, isolating herself totally wasn't in her best interest. She agreed, saying she really missed her relationships but she didn't see any way to get what she wanted from them and reject what she didn't want. I thought she could and I explained, "As a little child, you had a very special wisdom about life and I have a hunch that you can tap into that knowledge now to find the right way to let people know what you need and what you don't need. Also, you have a high degree of integrity. You seem to be doing what you have to do. I think you can make clear to your friends and your husband that you're in charge of your health – that you're doing what is necessary and that life does not need to stop. Obviously you want to go on living and enjoying life. And lastly your marvelous sense of humor, which has so often made my day can certainly be used to help make everyone comfortable again.

"But you're going to have to let these people know what you want. You must tell your friend who keeps giving you scientific information on breast cancer that this isn't what you need right now. Perhaps you encouraged her by asking so many questions that she felt responsible for your scientific knowledge."

Stephanie agreed. "Yes, as I look back, I can see that I definitely set her up for that." "As for your friend who is always serious, perhaps she doesn't understand your need for humor," I told Stephanie, "and as for your husband, he may be terribly frightened and really need assurance that not only are you planning to stay around, but that you have begun a life with him that you're truly enjoying."

The next week Stephanie came in smiling. Before she spoke I could see by her eager face that she had made some progress. She said, "I told each of them that I have intelligence, integrity and humor. Then I went on to explain what I meant. I told Marsha that I don't need her worrying about me and looking so serious. I need her to let me be funny, just like in the old days. Marsha tried to understand, but she said it was very hard because she saw humor as inappropriate when someone is dealing with a life threatening illness. My other friend said that she would try to take cues from me for giving me medical information. I came up with a great solution for my husband: I just said, 'Hon, put the newspaper down and come up to the bedroom and let's have some fun.' I decided that lovemaking would break the ice a lot better than a long analysis. I guess I was using 'wise woman' knowledge!"

Stephanie was struggling for comfortable connections to people while dealing with a life threatening illness. I made the therapeutic decision that this was not the time for her to withdraw from her most important supports, no more than it was a time for her to have unrealistically high expectations about positive states of mind. However, as we've learned from the extensive literature on and by AIDS patients, sometimes people have their most profound Enchanted Moments during a severe crisis. The intensity of the moment can mobilize positive resources and positive states of mind. Whether this would happen for Stephanie or not, I needed to help her relate successfully with loved ones and friends – she needed them now more than ever.

In terms of THE ENCHANTED SELF therapy, rather than talk to her about her old patterns of distancing when she was stressed, I emphasized her talents, which included wisdom, integrity and humor. I made it clear to her that she must signal each person about how she wants them to relate to her, and I helped her to see that she was in charge of her own physical and emotional needs.

Connie and Michael

Connie and Michael, a young professional couple in their late thirties, came to see me for some advice about having a second child. Connie, aware that her biological clock was running out, was eager to have another child. A successful businesswoman, she felt that she could manage any and all of the hassles and complications of life with two children. Michael wasn't so sure. He was ambivalent about a second child, saying that his ambivalence was based on the exhaustion they were already experiencing, transporting their little boy back and forth to the baby-sitters and adjusting work schedules when he was sick. Actually, Michael felt that their lives were quite frenzied. In frustration, each was moving to a more locked position. Connie became more certain that she could handle a second child; and Michael became more vehement that their married life was a shambles right now.

As the therapist trying to listen with that third ear, I told them that "there isn't much living time going on. There's family time, but it sounds frantic and exhausting." Michael immediately responded with a big smile and a softening of his face. "Yes, that's right," he said. "It's like we're never in a state of just being – like in Bob Dylan's song, 'We're not just being there. Yeah, I want to 'be three' before we're 'four.' I want us to just 'be there'."

Connie smiled, "I want those moments, too", she said, "and I think we have some good moments, like the other day, when I took our son, Donald, down to the lake early and we fed the ducks. It felt wonderful to me. That seemed like 'being there.' "

But Michael interrupted, saying, "Do you remember when I was looking for you at the lake? I came up and tried to join you and all you could say was, 'Is Donald's lunch ready? Is Donald's lunch pail packed' "?

Connie looked surprised. "I didn't realize that I hurt you by asking those questions. I was just being practical at that moment."

121

Michael seemed near tears, saying, "I wanted to join you, but I didn't feel you really wanted me to – I felt pushed away – I guess because you immediately started talking about chores. That hurt my feelings. I guess I don't always tell you when I'm hurt."

I said, "It seems as if the two of you need to take more time to just 'be there' with each other and Donald. Perhaps I can help teach you some of the skills that would make you less likely to misjudge the potentially good moments and not spoil them with a criticism or reminder or task."

Both Connie and Michael wanted more enhanced time in their lives as a family, but they hadn't learned how to effectively share their specific needs with each other. Connie was experiencing an Enchanted Moment with her little boy. She didn't realize that by becoming task oriented when Michael appeared, she spoiled his chance to join in. Michael hadn't been able to talk with Connie about his concerns that there wasn't enough "real" time in their marriage. Instead they became trapped in the issue of whether or not to have another child. He was ambivalent but not against a second child. What he was against was a life that didn't permit him enough time to enjoy his family.

During the next few sessions Connie and Michael were able to process further some of the dynamics mentioned above. One of their achievements was to be able to increase their enhanced time together as a family.

Tanya

Tanya, an engineer in her mid thirties, had been married for a year at the time she started her therapy with me. When she was a child, Tanya won many academic and sports awards, but because of her mother's poor health, she'd been brought up mostly by her grandparents who had many other obligations. Tanya often felt ignored. She became a survivor, taking care of herself.

Single for a long while, Tanya had adapted well to living alone and had developed many interests and friendships. By the time she married Roger she wasn't used to having someone around all the time, who would share decision-making. As much as Tanya had wished to marry, she understandably experienced anxiety and confusion around the decision. She was still anxious a year later. ENCHANTED SELF therapy centered around her efforts to sort through marriage issues, as well as social and personal issues.

Eventually she brought up the discrepancy between her and Roger's needs. For example, she noted, "Often he's in the mood to make love and is all ready while I still have a list of things I need to take care of. As a matter of fact, I think I need about three hours as a 'window' for making love. I guess I feel kind of guilty and confused about needing that time."

I asked Tanya why she needed three hours. She explained that she needed to unwind before the actual lovemaking and then wanted to nap afterwards. As she told it, it did seem that she needed three hours! My initial suggestion to her was that rather than feeling guilty, she accept the fact that this was her requirement. I suggested that she might express this to her husband so that he could under-stand her. Hopefully, they could figure out when they could put this three hour period into their lives.

Apparently, however, my releasing her from guilt and suggesting a plan was not adequate, for she went on to discuss how she had dif-ferent priorities on different days. Even on Saturday, which might have seemed like the most likely day, she worried that household chores wouldn't get done if they gave up three hours for love-making. What time would they eat dinner out?

I asked Tanya if perhaps there were some other issues going on that were creating difficulty in clearing enough time for intimacy. She pondered, then answered yes, she guessed so. She was angry because she was seeing a lot less of her friends than she used to. She felt disconnected from many of her relationships because of spending time with Roger, instead of with her friends, during their first year of marriage. As Tanya went on, she began to muse that perhaps not finding the time to make love was her way of expressing anger toward her husband. She said that she really felt she needed privacy and time out for herself as well as time to socialize with other people.

I suggested that rather than trying to discuss some of her needs with her husband, Tanya was creating an elaborate rationale for avoiding the topic. Tanya took to heart the assignment of communi-cating better with her husband, working on it for the next few weeks.

123

Like many contemporary young women, Tanya was attempting to balance her need for time for herself and her friends, her husband's needs for intimacy and her own decisions about the future. She was also attempting to set short and long term professional goals, trying to predict what demands would be made on her. I realized that the more Tanya could work out these needs and learn to express herself clearly to Roger rather than going underground, the better able she would be to handle her needs – social, professional and intimate – when she was no longer in therapy.

Happily, Tanya found the perfect opportunity to start talking more openly with her husband about their scheduling needs. One night she came home late to a fire in the fireplace and soft music playing. It seemed as if he had been waiting for her. Yet Roger said nothing, not even hello. Tanya was tired and went up to bed. Finally, he came upstairs and reminded her that she had promised to make love that night. Tanya did not respond and for the next several days they were silent. Finally, after much internal processing and anguish, she was able to talk to him in a way that he could hear. She told him that she'd been feeling distressed for days and apologized for having forgotten her pledge to make love but said she was hurt that he hadn't realized she had simply forgotten. Why couldn't he have tried to remind her instead of acting hurt and keeping silent when she came home? She felt as though he'd been testing her and that she'd failed the test. They talked this episode through with feelings being expressed and heard on both sides.

After this, they were able to decide to go out for an early dinner and then have plenty of time to make love. Tanya felt good that she'd been able to talk without attacking him and yet had really shared her feelings. She felt she had learned to assert herself in a positive, effective way with her husband. We continued to process some of the issues around her need for privacy and to control events rather than feeling comfortable with spontaneity. I suggested that her talent for time management could work to their advantage in vacation planning, chores and leisure time, rather than against them. During her last session, Tanya was eager to describe their agenda for a trip to Greece. She had researched and planned their itinerary carefully, with her husband's blessings. She commented, "It's great to see I can use my skills and not feel my needs are being disregarded. I've even built in two open times during the week — four hours each for us in bed!"

Theresa

I would like to end this chapter with a vignette about a young married woman, Theresa, who was brought up in a very protected, restrictive home where she was unable to develop successful negotiating skills. She had became a highly anxious adult who felt guilty if she dared to make any type of assertive remark, no matter how appropriate.

In one session she discussed how she had gone with her husband to his father's home. While they were there he and his father got into an argument about his younger brother, who had committed a delinquent act. She felt there was justification for anger, but her husband and his father were speaking disparagingly about the brother while he was in the next room. Theresa felt pained knowing that the youngster was hearing such negative comments and nothing positive. Since she herself had had some problems of a similar nature years earlier, she felt a bond with the brother. At the same time, she found him difficult herself and could understand the men's anger. She was conflicted about her own feelings. She tried to signal to her husband to stop the discussion, but he told her to leave him alone. At that point, she felt herself cower and go into her shell. Later, as they drove home, she felt depressed.

Theresa told me that she always cowers when her husband yells at her or at anyone else. Even when he is not yelling, he can easily deflate her and make her feel like a victim. She said, "It's so hard to have the strength to try to negotiate with him because he knows exactly what he believes in and he is so righteous! He's forceful and sincere, even cocky." While her husband knows exactly what he wants, often Theresa is unsure of what she wants. He doesn't see all sides of an issue the way she does, nor does he feel guilty about speaking up for himself.

I did two interventions with Theresa, one standard and one that came spontaneously. First, I gave her some concrete suggestions as to how she might have shared some of her feelings with her husband on the way home from his father's house. I suggested that she might

125

have shared how nervous and upset the public display of anger had made her feel. She might also have reminded him that he has a lot of good advice and insight, but that when he attacks someone by verbal abuse, he doesn't come across to his advantage. She could also have explained that his behavior triggered bad memories in her, making her feel frightened, as if she were the victim, leading to depression. She might have asked him to talk directly to his younger brother, using more neutral language, or discuss issues more quietly with his father so that the brother wouldn't overhear. Theresa agreed, but all that seemed hard for her to put into action, she said.

I listened and realized that my suggested interventions may have made sense but were not timely for her. Then I had a spontaneous idea. Thinking back, I believe I was responding to Theresa's animated manner, seeing her energy level, her facial and hand gestures, her bright penetrating eyes as communicating assets. I asked Theresa to close her eyes and imagine that she was giving Danny feedback and sharing her feelings and thoughts. I told her not to think of the exact words, but just to think the feelings of being able to say what she needed to say, trying not to feel anxious. I asked her to imagine positive emotions successfully in her fantasy. Perhaps she did not know what to say in real life and did not feel she could try new behaviors yet, but I wanted her to practice by visualizing expressing her thoughts and feelings. Theresa closed her eyes and I could see them move. Her hands also moved a little as she appeared to go through the process of telling Danny exactly how she felt, in pantomime. Then she opened her eyes. I asked her if she felt she had gotten her point across. She said, "I'm not really satisfied. Can I do it again?" This time, her head moved frequently. She smiled. She was obviously living each stage of sharing with Danny. She signaled with her hands more often and more expressively than the first time. Finally, she opened her eyes and said, "Yes, I think I got my point across."

Theresa left the session smiling and looking relaxed. As she walked out, she said, "I'm glad we tried that. It was a very different way of giving myself some sense of empowerment. I don't know if I can do it yet at home with Danny, but it still felt good to be able to express myself."

As I instructed Theresa in the visualization, I made clear to her that I accepted the fact and appreciated her honesty in saying that she could not incorporate my pragmatic verbal suggestions in her discussion with her husband, even though they made sense to her.

Summary

In this chapter we have looked at how difficult it is to experience THE ENCHANTED SELF if we don't learn adequately how to get our needs met. Reasons why THE ENCHANTED SELF technique could be helpful in encouraging clients to learn how to meet their needs as well as case studies illustrating therapeutic teaching opportunities were presented.

Reader's exercise

Pick three different types of personal encounters that you have had or are likely to have: one where you are always successful; one where you are moderately successful; and one where you have had difficulty. Each time, I'd like you to close your eyes and imagine yourself, as Theresa did, handling an encounter by visualizing it. Don't worry about language. Just see yourself effectively handling the situation. Imagine yourself saying what you want to express. Start with an easy encounter, the one you always succeed at, then go on to the moderate encounter and, finally, to a difficult one. Stay with each visualization, repeating it, if necessary, until you know you have succeeded. Jot down how you feel once you have accomplished these three levels of negotiating. What strengths did you exhibit? For example, did you keep yourself from crying or raising your voice? Did your words just roll out like quicksilver? Did you use your hands or body language effectively? Give yourself a pat on the back for whatever talents emerged during these three visualizations. Don't worry about whether or not you can use them yet.

Chapter Ten

THE SONG OF THE SOUL

What is the SONG OF THE SOUL?

As I've noted, there seems to be an almost magical quality to the reintegration of Positive Fingerprints of the Mind and/or Shadow Prints of the Mind, into current positive states of being, what I call THE ENCHANTED SELF. As we begin to practice the retrieval and the maintenance of positive states of being, as we do our homework separating out the dysfunctional from the functional parts of our past, as we strengthen our self-worth, as we find more successful ways to get our needs met, we enter a new threshold. This threshold is the gateway to THE SONG OF THE SOUL. All the therapeutic work we and our clients have done will eventually result in accessing what is most unique and specifically enhancing about the self. Individuals can now access their talents, imaginations, interpersonal skills, passions, preferences and knowledge. All of these capacities will have tremendous energy behind them as they burst forward into the present, released from the negative forces experienced earlier in life, such as mislabeling and lack of support. What remains is the golden-nugget of personal potential freed from negative interference. In the best of all worlds if you could see a person singing her SONG OF THE SOUL, you'd see someone fully aware of her talents and strengths; a person who thinks highly of herself and has the ability to negotiate for what she wants and needs. She can feel valuable and important whether her life is public or private. Her self-esteem would come from an inner sense of harmony with her own spirit rather than from external validation.

Of course, what I'm talking about is the ideal and just as we never reach infinity we do not reach the full SONG OF OUR SOULS every moment of our lives. However, as we develop positive regard for ourselves, practice positive states of being and learn how to have our needs met, we begin to sing our SONG OF THE SOUL at least some of the time. While THE ENCHANTED SELF is a positive state of being that incorporates aspects of a person's uniqueness, THE SONG OF THE SOUL is a form of "being."

Imagine the following: Tara, busy mother and homemaker, stands in the kitchen with a pile of dishes in front of her. Suddenly she looks out of the window and sees a beautiful sunset. She puts down her rubber gloves, turns off the water and lets her mind wander to some wonderful feelings she had at Girl Scout camp as she stood at the edge of the lake watching the sunset. She finds herself feeling a pleasant warmth and sense of well-being. She makes a cup of tea and sits down at her kitchen table still gazing at the beautiful sunset. Relaxed and comforted by positive feelings from her past she lingers in this delightful moment. When her husband comes to the door to ask her to find something he's missing, she calmly answers that she will be available in fifteen minutes.

This example shows a woman able to experience her ENCHANTED SELF. About to do an ordinary chore she is stimulated by a beautiful image retrieving some positive memories. These positive Fingerprints and Shadowprints of the Mind help her return to a serene state of well-being. In this state she is able to get her own needs met, e.g., she tells her husband to wait fifteen minutes. She feels enough self-esteem to permit herself a delay in her household chores and she's been able to get in touch with her unique memory bank in a positive way.

Let's look at this scenario: Mary, wife and homemaker with several young children, lived on a farm growing up. She has a keen love of nature. Living in a suburban area she proudly keeps a compost pile in her back yard and a small vegetable garden grows in her side yard.

Herbs are growing in trays in the kitchen and in the pantry are homemade canned goods. The children also have a tiny plot where they are growing flowers and vegetables of their choice. Many of the children's books are stories about farm life or rural living. The older child, Greg, age nine, is a member of a 4-H Club, even though his mother must drive him twenty miles to participate in its activities. The family's summer vacations have centered around visits to national wildlife preserves and/or staying at farm homes, either with people whom Mary has stayed in contact with from childhood or on occasion, paid-for lodgings. Mary's sense of the sacred in nature is apparent in her charity canisters on the kitchen table where she throws in change every day for the SPCA and THE WILD LIFE FUND. Even insects are treated with respect in her house. The children are taught to bring them outside when found in the wrong places. The natural rhythm of life is important to Mary and she often encourages the children and her husband to sit with her on the deck while the sun is setting. She loves the way she feels as they sit together in the twilight, just as she sat on the front porch with her parents in Arkansas – centered, safe and "at home" at a profound level.

During this time she tells stories about growing up on the farm – when the favorite cow had twins and the veterinarian had to come in the middle of the night; how they kept the two calves as milking cows; when all the chickens were lost in a fire; when the blind barn cat disappeared and was found two weeks later proudly trailing behind her five kittens. Often her husband, who grew up in the city, interjects his stories of growing up on the streets of Hoboken. The sunset hours have become a beautiful ritual of family life.

Mary's story not only illustrates her capacity to achieve positive states of being. We also recognize that she is able to access a SONG OF HER SOUL. She's found a way to have her needs met. She is able to utilize positive memories from her own childhood; and she has enough self-esteem to feel entitled to utilize and enjoy these capacities. However, beyond this, we perceive, in the way she's living, Mary's value system, her ethics, her preferences, her interests and her talents, as well as her love of family. Her SONG OF THE SOUL is not the result of a one time positive state of mind or body. Mary has woven into much of her lifestyle, again and again, not only permission to experience her ENCHANTED SELF but beyond that a commitment to bring into her family life a sense of her deep love and respect of nature.

Thus, THE SONG OF THE SOUL actually carries within it our traits, talents, hopes, desires and self-knowledge, and thrusts them forward in a kind of hologram of one's uniqueness and one's purpose. Just as a hologram appears to move and make a composite, three dimensional image from any direction, so can one's SONG OF THE SOUL shift and appear to emphasize different aspects of one's core self, dependent on the circumstances. Thus if Mary is busy canning stringbeans from her garden, that may reveal a different emphasis of herself than when she is telling her children and her husband as they watch the sunset about the time when all the neighbors pitched in to build new chicken coops on her farm after a fire.

Metaphorically, THE SONG OF THE SOUL is a cross between one's fingerprints that never change over a lifetime, except in size, and one's baby picture, which shows a certain resemblance in configuration of features, eye color, skin tone, etc., to one's adult picture. They are somewhat the same but not identical. Mary's love of nature went back to earliest childhood. However, the way she incorporates that love, singing her SONG OF THE SOUL as an adult living in a suburban neighborhood, is very different from its expression had she remained in a rural setting. So, too, emphases shift as we become adults. Protection of nature was not on Mary's mind as a child, nor was passing on a commitment of nature to others. Now it is.

Accessing THE SONG OF THE SOUL

A person can easily achieve an Enchanted state of being through a workshop experience or when appropriately guided by a teacher or therapist. But we do not know if the effect will last beyond that actual experience. For example, I could help someone learn square dancing after ascertaining that she had some interest in movement and dance in her childhood. Later she might recall learning to square dance as an ENCHANTED SELF episode. However, she may not intensely identify herself with square dancing. Square dancing happened to be useful as a vehicle to obtain a positive state of being for the person. Although it was based on real memory retrieval, it was not central to that person's disposition or personality. Thus, for her, THE ENCHANTED

SELF square dancing moment may be alive, but then die. This doesn't mean that it has no value. Just the practice of learning how to stimulate positive states of mind and/or body can be extremely useful and healthy. However, as I showed with Mary's example, one's SONG OF THE SOUL is not a one time positive state of mind or body. Rather, it is a function of one's value system, preferences and interest, talents and potential, subculture and family and, ultimately, one's purpose in life. Unfortunately for many of us, we cannot gain access to our SONG OF THE SOUL because of the confounding messages we received in childhood that distort and confuse our intuitive sense of who we are and what we're all about. But the therapist who uses THE ENCHANTED SELF technique can very effectively help her client get through to what is most authentic about herself.

Yet therapists may discover that their clients will not or cannot necessarily work with them to clarify their SONG OF THE SOUL. More likely, they'll share their self-knowledge indirectly, or possibly, not until later on in therapy. Ultimately, THE SONG OF THE SOUL is based on deep insight and self-wisdom. We clinicians help sift though the past, we strengthen self-regard, we teach arbitration skills, we help clients recognize and encourage positive states of mind. However we are not always with them during the "aha" moment that signals their recognition of THE SONG OF THE SOUL. That often takes place during a private moment when she feels especially wise and deep. You will see in the case studies described later in this chapter that so often clients bring the diamond, already polished, into the therapy room. But you will note, too, that we may be so involved in sifting through the dysfunction, that we may not see the diamond glimmering right before our eyes! That is why I describe many different ways clients let me know about their SONG OF THE SOUL.

Tragically, many SONGS OF THE SOUL are never sung. One of my clients mentioned recently that she remembered a great sense of triumph at age three when she finished reading a story to herself after her mother abruptly left her bedside. She even defined the memory as an Enchanted Moment. But her high-achieving parents gave her no particular credit, since they expected her to be advanced. Neither did her early reading win praise at school because she was way ahead of the class and had usually read the current

133

book. Her teachers often criticized her for looking inattentive. So she had no positive identity around her early triumphs. The moment was hers but it was not useful in forming her adult SONG OF THE SOUL or in giving her much pleasure when she looked back at it. To paraphrase a Torah commentator, "If we are not heard and we do not give language to what happens it is of no use." To the Zen Buddhist's question of "What would be the sound of one hand clapping?" I would reply that whatever the sound, it would not be a Song; it would not have the potential to be a SONG OF THE SOUL until there were two hands clapping. By that I mean we help each other by reinforcing, naming and acknowledging each other's talents and our moments of elation. Thus we give them value. We cannot sing a SONG OF THE SOUL in isolation.

How I discovered THE SONG OF THE SOUL

I first became aware of what I later called THE SONG OF THE SOUL after many interviews with women during which some talked about favorite hobbies, pleasures, or special capacities, while others seemed to be expressing a central theme around positive aspects of their lives. Some seemed to be living a multifaceted life that clearly demonstrated earlier talents and interests, rebirthed in adult fashion, combined with purpose and commitment. I sensed each women's deeply felt personal philosophy and her commitment to self and others, combined with her impressive capacity for positive states of well being. Because the interviews were brief, I may have missed qualities of THE SONG OF THE SOUL in some of the women interviewed. However, I discovered, while not even looking for THE SONG OF THE SOUL, that many of the women lived restorative lives – that is, lives that seemed to correct earlier dysfunctions and incorporated earlier hopes and potential in ways that gave them a sense of purpose and a continuing narrative. I knew that I was seeing more than what I called THE ENCHANTED SELF. Here are some examples:

Sally

Sally, forty-eight, is a self-employed windowfitter and Jack-of-all-Trades. She was raised as the prodigy of brilliant physicians. Sally grew up in a formal household with exquisitely high standards for achievement and manners. She felt emotionally burdened by her environment, experiencing it as cold and unreceptive to her emotional needs. Determined as an adult to live a more natural and even rugged life, Sally and her husband built their own home in Nebraska. Although she stayed home to care for her children, she often sat in the local diner holding court. In these meetings she taught the local construction workers her trades. Many told her they'd never before had an opportunity to be appreciated or listened to as they talked about their work. She helped them solve construction problems, coming up with new ideas for them and supporting their self-esteem. In addition to her meetings with them, she applied the perfectionism learned in childhood to carving beautiful wooden barrettes. This craft not only gave her artistic pleasure, but helped her reconnect with the party clothes and fancy hairdos she had liked in her youth.

I perceived a sense of purpose in her conversations with the workmen and a philosophy of life in crafting the barrettes. It seemed to me that she wanted to live a more natural life now than she could in her formal childhood. However, in adult life she carried with her from childhood the need to achieve on many levels and to share her accomplishments. So I felt that her creativity and her didactic breakfasts were reflections of her ENCHANTED SELF, and also suggest her SONG OF THE SOUL.

Phyllis

In her early seventies, Phyllis, in one brief interview, shared many aspects of what I consider her SONG OF THE SOUL. She mentioned how happy she was. After a recent divorce, she had settled into her own apartment and lifestyle. She equipped her kitchen to prepare the health food she likes and, in the living room, placed her sewing machine and piano. She told me that she becomes so attached to the dresses she makes that she can't throw them away. Instead, she alters them to fit her changing figure. She goes to the Jewish Community Center on the senior citizens' bus and learns folk dances. She described how she sings and laughs with the others. "We're just like young girls. You know, I'm really happier than I ever was. When my cousin in Spain called, I said to her, 'I'm not the same person that you knew. I can't believe how different I am. I'm really experiencing joy. I do what I want and I go where I want. I'm doing all the things I always wanted to do.'"

What a contrast to her life as a wife, when she'd been timid and exhausted, she said. She'd worked hard at motherhood and never had any sense of herself or time for herself. In her marriage she never felt that her husband was responsive or appreciative. He put her down and accused her of showing off if she wore one of the dresses she'd made for herself. When the children were fully grown, she made the decision to separate from her emotionally stingy man. She considers her new life to be a rebirth.

When I asked Phyllis about her childhood, she mentioned having lived a very simple rural life in Spain. She most remembered being part of a warm family, and considered family life essential to her identity. She learned to sew and cook, embroider and play the piano. When she married at twenty-six, she really didn't know her husband well and when she got to know him, after marriage, she didn't feel that he was what she really wanted. But her inner voice told her to be patient. She considered that this was her inner wisdom directing her and it proved to be the turning point for her. She was patient and left only when she considered the time to be right.

To me, Phyllis represents a women singing her SONG OF THE SOUL because she was able to integrate so many aspects of her being: her creative passions, her philosophy of life, her health and her sense of self-worth. She was also able to find the time and emotional space for them. All of these factors came together for Phyllis so that she flourished. Not only was she singing her SONG OF THE SOUL every day but she was able to access energy that I doubt would have been available to her if she had not been so in tune with herself.

Almost as an afterthought Phyllis mentioned something that had happened recently. She rents a modest apartment near her children. The landlord had sent a letter requesting a rent increase. She was terribly upset and wrote him back, indicating that the apartment was perfect for her, that she was an older woman just barely getting by. She said she couldn't afford the increase. Her landlord wrote back within the week telling her that he would leave the rent as it was for the year. He, too, had a mother! It struck me as fascinating that

Phyllis, who talked about herself in younger days as timid, had in her seventies challenged her landlord successfully.

Phyllis had achieved her SONG OF THE SOUL because she was able to utilize the three dimensions discussed in Chapter VIII, again and again. The chart on p. 94 shows us how as we practice positive states of being, improved self esteem and getting our needs met, we are better able to access our ENCHANTED SELVES. This leads, as we become more and more equipped in these three dimensions, to the expression of our SONG OF THE SOUL. Phyllis had brought forth many talents and interests from her childhood and was able to weave them appropriately into her senior years. She was also able to improve her self-esteem. It took approximately thirty years for her to develop a sense of self-worth that finally permitted her to say "no" to her marriage and to exit successfully. Now, in her later years, she was able to meet her personal needs. She had proportioned time for self development, time with her family and time to listen to her inner wisdom which helped her to become her own guide.

This inner wisdom is something that I believe lies within each of us. To access it, however, takes, as Phyllis said, "patience and time." We need to know what will balance our lives and we need to feel worthy of the life we want. This will give us access to positive states of being – and we'll begin to sing *our* SONG OF THE SOUL.

Discovering my own SONG OF THE SOUL

When I discovered my SONG OF THE SOUL and through it a broader understanding of women's wisdom, I felt a profound sense of destiny. I saw that my life had meaning, that it was not trivial. I'd finally made contact with important parts of myself, where once I'd felt shame or discomfort. Instead, I experienced strength, courage, determination, optimism and the certainty that my mission was credible and, therefore, so was I. I sensed that perhaps I had the makings of an heroic figure in my own time, as I now believe we all have – if we can approach our SONG OF OUR SOUL. Tuning in to one's "self" is as delicate and exquisite as fine-tuning a harp. Only we, ourselves, know when the pitch is absolutely correct. Even if our lives seem terrific, in the eyes of someone else – an adoring husband, responsive children, friends, a boss – there may still be a shadow or corner that somehow does not feel right.

For me, the final "aha" moment that gave me access to my unique strengths did not come in my therapy but, as I described in Chapter II, after a long personal journey. Only after finally defining myself as a divinely empowered person with inner wisdom and great capacities for self-development – with the ability to help others develop – only then could I stand on the threshold of my SONG OF THE SOUL. My self-discovery required not only therapy, but also other experiences: interviewing women, my emergency surgery, and certain other events described in Chapter II which led to my spiritual study of what it means to be a woman.

Often, of course, I was able to realize when I felt creative, bright, in control and genuinely devoted to others. But even with therapy I was never able to find the combination of traits that I could most proudly call "me." Too often I labeled positive traits "masculine," and rejected them in myself.

As I think back I've pondered why the labels of "masculine-feminine" were so important to me. I think there were several reasons. One was that my extended family valued "feminine" characteristics such as submissiveness, acquiescence, prettiness, dutifulness. Although I certainly wanted to be pretty, I found the other characteristics to be dangerous. They seemed to threaten a woman's spirit. Yet in my own home, I was encouraged to be bright and achieving. What then kept me from overriding the extended family's narrow sense of womanhood? Two factors: My father as an educator, encouraged my mother, a homemaker with a high school degree, to develop professionally. With his support and encouragement she attended college and received her Masters degree in Education, becoming a beloved second and third grade teacher for many years. However, within the family, my father often "put down" my mother. I was emotionally more comfortable identifying with my father. I felt confused by his criticisms of my mother and they negatively influenced me. I found it harder to identify with my mother's talents; her ability to tell amazing stories, her sense of humor, her love of color and style, her interest in people's comings and goings, her intuitive perceptions about those people, and her social finesse, including entertaining.

Perhaps I felt I had abandoned my mother by wishing to emulate my father's style and power in the outside world. Perhaps I felt guilty for not being able to really value my mother for her talents, not understanding that my father's criticisms had interfered with my identifying with my mother. Whatever the reasons, the definitions of 'masculine' and 'feminine' traits became distorted and emotionally laden in dysfunctional ways for me. My childhood home left me with difficulties in getting close to what was most authentic about myself.

Understanding the ancient concept of the feminine as "A divinely empowered person with infinite inner wisdom"[20] suddenly made it easy for me to identify those experiences that had been most self-enhancing and authentic in my youth. For example, being on the Student Council in fourth grade was a positive experience, giving me the chance to see that I had leadership capacities. I loved wearing my safety patrol belt and voting on school programs. I felt power when I became an excellent reader and was often called on to read to the class during rest hour. I also experienced competency playing the violin, as well as in writing poetry and taking care of my dolls. In looking back to childhood I recognize authenticity in my capacity to make friends, play and socialize.

As an adolescent, I was thrilled to belong to youth groups and see now that this was reflective of social and cultural talents as well as a genuine commitment to helping make the world a better place. I was smart, I was radiant, I was full of life. I saw that I could handle friendships and love interests and could make important indepen-dent decisions and even hear my voice of inner wisdom. For example, the night after a long day of excruciating pain, I made a decision not to use a hot water bottle on my stomach. Only the next day, after I'd arrived at the hospital and my appendix had been removed, did the doctors tell us that if I had used heat on my stomach, my appendix would have burst during the night. My inner wisdom had saved me.

Ultimately, as a teenager, I found I had negotiating skills and a capacity to get my own needs met within my own family. I remem-ber one day telling my parents clearly why many of their arguments were unnecessary and destructive to each other. I talked long and clearly and my parents were hushed, as if amazed at my ability to put into words what they had really been doing all those years. After that, in my opinion, there began to be a profound improvement in the emotional climate of our home. And indeed, the years have actually turned a young couple with poor negotiating skills into two sea-soned lovers, wisely aware that there are enough conflicts in life without their adding to them. Their home has become harmonious and their respect for each other apparent.

As I continued to look back on my life and began to be able to sort through my talents, strengths and potential, based on the sense of my authenticity as a person rather than getting lost in masculine/feminine labels, I began truly to love the little girl whom I had been, and the bright teenager from whom a woman was emerging. I needed my journey in adulthood, a complex spiral of experiences that included several psychotherapies and a health crisis, to help me discover MY SONG OF THE SOUL.

Getting in touch with THE SONG OF THE SOUL

It is very possible to start to sing one's SONG OF THE SOUL in a particular area of one's life, but still to be dysfunctional in other areas. It is natural to see in our clients, as well as in ourselves, changes that lead to self-integration, self-validation, integrity of spirit and commitment in one area of life, and yet to see problems remaining in other areas. However, like fine tuning a violin or a cello, the more one becomes aware of being "in tune," the more chance one has of expanding one's SONG OF THE SOUL to include these other dimensions.

Remember Tara who was looking out the window watching the sunset, pausing to retrieve some positive memories and have a cup of tea? She had achieved an ENCHANTED SELF state of being. However, even though she'd found a way to meet her needs and valued herself enough to take this time, we do not know whether shortly after she'd become overwhelmed by interruptions. Perhaps she might handle these in a way that would lead her to violate her private space. As we begin to sing our SONG OF THE SOUL, as Mary did, we note a respect for our authenticity that goes beyond the immediate. Again and again, Mary was able to get back to her core values, talents and beliefs. However, there still may be dimensions in Mary's life where she has not been able to integrate her many attributes at the level of THE SONG OF THE SOUL. For example, perhaps the two days a week she works as a librarian are filled with problems with co-workers or supervisors. She may have less self-esteem while at that job. Perhaps she feels used and abused and she comes home with hurt feelings, on the verge of tears.

In that case, how is it that Mary was able to sing her SONG OF THE SOUL in her domestic life, yet at the job couldn't get her needs met, and felt terrible about herself? It would seem that she doesn't yet have the negotiating skills necessary to achieve a sense of well-being on this job, or perhaps those with whom she works aren't responsive to her needs, no matter how well she expresses them. Perhaps she finds herself trapped there for one reason or another, such as a scarcity of other jobs in her community for someone of her background and education, or because of her particular scheduling requirements. All through our lives we take on many roles and identities, as we saw that Mary did. Like her, in some of our roles we're more successful than in others. Often we know how to get our needs met, feel good about ourselves and achieve positive states of being in one role but not in another. Billy, age 15, may be successful as a friend but not know how to navigate to his benefit as a student.

In each sphere of a person's life one has the opportunity to sing a SONG OF THE SOUL. Each person has many SONGS OF THE SOUL waiting to be sung or being sung, and yet there is also a potential for one general harmonic SONG OF THE SOUL. The violins play my SONG OF THE SOUL in terms of my role as a wife. The wind instruments are playing my SONG OF THE SOUL in terms of my role as a friend. The horns are playing my SONG OF THE SOUL as I work at my profession. The flutes resonate THE SONG OF THE SOUL in my spiritual journey. Each comes together to make the music of a fully orchestrated· piece of music, i.e., my SONG OF THE SOUL. Of course, each instrument will not necessarily play the same notes, nor will any of the various instruments sound alike. And if the violins are out of tune, or even one clarinet hits a sour note, it will affect the quality of my whole symphony.

The therapist's roles in THE SONG OF THE SOUL

As the therapist, you may only hear of a client's SONG OF THE SOUL once she has begun singing it in a particular dimension of her life. The client may grow in therapy, dealing with the issues she brings to the office, and then leap ahead suddenly integrating her wisdom in a self-enhancing unique way when you're not around. Your power as a therapist is in teaching your client how to transfer positive behaviors from her SONG OF THE SOUL to more and more facets of her life. For example, if somebody has started to truly fly in all dimensions at the office, what talents and strengths is she exhibiting? How can these be best understood and transferred to helping her SONG OF THE SOUL emerge in her home situation or perhaps in a significant relationship? This is where your therapeutic knowledge and background helps.

Let's look at Mary again and imagine that she's your client. You have applauded and validated her ability to sing her SONG OF SOUL at home. However, as noted, she's still bothered by her feelings of despair at work. You encourage her to recognize and celebrate the talents she has utilized in singing her SONG OF THE SOUL at home. You suggest ways she might use these talents at work. You also help her to work through self-esteem issues that seem to make her more vulnerable to her supervisors at work than to her children and husband. Now you help her envision a way that she can utilize her particular talents and strengths to assert herself more successfully at work. Does she have any positive memories she can retrieve? This may require your help in sorting through functional from dysfunctional areas in her past. As a child, she may have had successes earning pocket money or doing well in school, or dealing with strangers in town. These memories of competency probably could be utilized to help her achieve a positive state of mind in her adult work environment.

Transferring positive learning

As Mary can transfer knowledge gleaned from areas of her life where she is so able to sing her SONG OF THE SOUL to other areas, such as her job, her full SONG OF THE SOUL will emerge. Her entire being will resonate harmonically from morning to night. Obviously, we pay a price emotionally and probably physically when we spend part of our lives in arenas where we feel unsuccessful, where our needs have not been met, where we experience self-esteem wounds and thus are not able to achieve positive states of being. However, with training it is possible to build upon good memories and strengths and make an intolerable situation more pleasant.

Please remember that THE ENCHANTED SELF therapy requires that the therapist augment the person's strengths rather than pointing out weaknesses. Thus we move from successful areas to areas that need help, accessing strengths, talents and potentials. Keep in mind that you want to help her cultivate, not plow under the fertile soil that gives life to her SONG OF THE SOUL. The therapist's attitude of mutuality and respect, combined with her absolute belief in her client's capacity to grow, promote the emergence of THE SONG OF THE SOUL. Fear of violation, even of the most minor nature, may keep a client from exploring her most innermost potential. Clear, positive, appropriately active involvement from the therapist and constantly watching the client's reaction to see if the therapist's communications are well tolerated, promote this process. These are far more effective than the classic passive "blank wall" stance. Because one client's violation may be another client's stimulus, the art of observation is key. Even when pointing out the client's strengths rather than weaknesses, the clinician must still remain a keen monitor of timing, pacing and the client's tolerance. In THE ENCHANTED SELF technique, criticisms are seldom given. However, when negative feedback must be given, try to couch the information within positive feedback. It is often safer and more in the client's interest to wait until talents have had more time to resurface, strengths have been rekindled and there is trust in the therapist's good will, before one points out certain weaknesses.

Now let us look at a variety of cases. Some of them illustrate where the first glimmer of a SONG OF THE SOUL is emerging, and some show the client who is well along in the singing of the SONG OF THE SOUL.

Kay – a slice of life as THE SONG OF THE SOUL

"Our vacation to the Bahamas was filled with family bickering, but I'm proud of myself that every night as the sun set I was able to get out my sketch pad and draw my impressions. I didn't allow family shit to get in the way of this wonderful part of me that I've retrieved from the past. I was able to hold onto it when we got home, even though I misplaced my wallet and I couldn't get organized and the kitchen was a mess! I stayed up that night, anyway, got out my paints and put in some personal art time. I love being able finally to say that I own my own talent and no one, whether or not they mean to, can interfere with it, or take it away from me again."

This brief testament to the SONG OF THE SOUL shows how it begins to emerge. Kay, a busy mother of four, obviously in a far from perfect marriage was, nonetheless, able to assert ownership of her artistic talent. My job as her therapist was to reinforce her ownership of her artistic talent, applaud it and enjoy it with her, while still continuing our multi-faceted therapy work so that her Song would eventually comprise more of her being.

Frank – when the emerging SONG OF THE SOUL enhances therapy

Frank, a good looking businessman in his late forties, had entered treatment because of feelings of depression. He and his wife fought all the time and had little successful communication. He was discouraged about his marriage and his business dealings and commented that he did not feel "at home" in any of his worlds. His early sessions focused on finding and documenting his talents and strengths as well as teaching Frank better negotiating skills. As I took his history, I applauded

Frank for having been able to handle well his dominating, demanding mother, the loss of his father when Frank was a teenager, and early job failures.

Frank's depressive symptoms lifted within a few months. Frank's wife came with him to several sessions, but she did not see therapy as relevant to her growth. Therapy continued individually.

One evening Frank came into his session looking very upbeat. He exclaimed, "I really feel whole!" I said, "Great," and asked him what he meant by that. He said, "I still have all my old issues but I feel great. I feel I've come together as a person. I have a sense of wholeness even though my wife, Sheila, and I have the same old problems. We've been competitive with each other forever, never really supporting each other emotionally in the small and big ways that couples should. But even so, my motivations are more real and honest and that's why I feel more whole. Even though I find myself automatically still behaving in ways that I wish I didn't, the force behind the behaviors is not coming from the old places anymore. I feel different inside. It's as if I've gotten myself back. For many years I gave up more than I got. I tried to become the image of what I thought a father and husband should be. I tried to build my marriage based on an image and it didn't work. I'm not false anymore. Not only do I feel whole, but I have a sense of my own power. Although my marriage is very difficult for me, I'm happier than I've ever been in my life and I'm more actively engaged in my life. Not only am I in graduate school and taking tennis lessons, but I have some great male friends."

I reinforced Frank's sense of wholeness enthusiastically. My excitement showed in my tone of voice and energy level. I reinforced the notion that the sense of wholeness he felt would strengthen him in all areas of his life. I also explained that he had more chance to break bad habits that still interfered with his marriage now that his motivations were coming from a place of integrity rather than from distorted notions of the male image. I applauded his new-found selfhood and his attempt to lead a richer, fuller life. At the same time, I suggested that progress could yet be made in the most dysfunctional area of his life – his marriage.

A month or so later, Frank came in, again elated. "I had the most wonderful vacation week," he beamed. "I got together with my buddies and played in a major tennis tournament; I even finished my extra project on my master's thesis. Then on Friday, Sheila and I were supposed to go to New York for the weekend but we had a fight. Finally, I said to her, "This is ridiculous, we're fighting and I don't really feel comfortable with you right now. Let's not go to New York. Maybe tomorrow – maybe the day after. She didn't feel well anyway, fighting a cold, so she went to bed early. The next day I went to New York by myself. I went to the Museum of Natural History and had a wonderful time. No one bothered me. I sat around, took my time and ate a nice lunch in the cafe. You know how much I love pre-historic stuff. I really was in heaven. Then, the next day, we decided to go to New York together. Tempers had cooled; we were both calm. Of course, it wasn't perfect. Sheila wouldn't give me clear signals as to what she wanted to do, but I took over and led her to the Museum. We had a nice day topped off by dinner in a Greek restaurant. She wouldn't tell me what she felt like eating, so I ordered and then we both realized that I had ordered something that she didn't like. I asked her if she wanted to change one of the dishes and she said "No." I didn't nag; she's a grown woman. We topped off the evening with a Broadway show.

Frank next described a really remarkable insight. "I was sitting in the sales-room at work and suddenly I had an "aha" moment. I realized that I'm definitely not a salesman. It's not for me. I love managing and that's what I should be doing. I've been trying to fit myself into the wrong role for years and years. I guess this is just the last in a series of "ahas" I now see that I tried to become a salesman because I thought that was the best road to making money. My dad had been a traveling salesman and I'd swallowed his definitions about what a father should be and what a husband should be. Now I see that all these definitions were killing my soul. I seem to have lots of energy and I'm already starting to think about new job opportunities in middle management. I think there might be a spot for me in my company, particularly because I'm taking the right courses."

I congratulated Frank for being able to change old behavior patterns in his marriage. I reminded him that just a month ago we'd talked about how difficult it can be to change. Now, just four weeks later, Frank had already come back with evidence of his capacity to break through old patterns regarding his work role. With wisdom and creativity he'd orchestrated a good weekend with Sheila, a weekend that in the past might have turned into a nightmare. In terms of his career, I wondered if the week's vacation he gave himself mobilized his creative insight about the work he really wanted to do. Perhaps all the positive things that he'd done on vacation, playing tennis with friends, working on his project, dealing more constructively with Sheila, seeing a musical, going to the museum he loved, released the energy he needed to see his career in a new way. Obviously he was ready to take an honest measure of himself. His thoughts about his work life showed a profound understanding of how he had been caught up in role definitions rather than really taking his unique needs and preferences into account.

The session ended with his describing how learning about Far Eastern religions had shown him the value of being in the moment, which he felt our culture did not pay enough attention to. Somehow, being wholly "present" in the moment gave him a sense that he could get out of his rut, that he would no longer have to "fit" a mold. He gave himself permission to retrieve his soul. Taking time for himself gave him a sense of personhood, which simply acting out role expectations did not. Living in our culture put great strain on Frank as he constantly felt obligated to be a good provider, a good husband, a good father, without a clear sense of his own inner self. Frank needed to step away in terms of some of our cultural values in order to find a way for his new identity to emerge more clearly. Being in the moment gave him a way to finally be "at home."

Frank is an example of someone who is on his way to singing his SONG OF THE SOUL. While it is true that his life is still troubled, in that his marriage and his work still cause him pain and he's distressed when he feels the tension between the mold he's set for himself in each major sphere in his life and the new emergence of his authentic self, I see him as much better off. He's like a sparrow learning to fly – starting to use his wings. Sometimes he's soaring, as he certainly was this past week.

For Frank, finding his SONG OF THE SOUL required separating out his assumptions of what a man "should" be from what fit his own personality, including his favorite hobbies, interests and preferences. He also needed to develop better negotiating skills as well as to have a willingness to accept help in transferring these skills from more successful to less successful areas of life. Sometimes finding one's SONG OF THE SOUL motivates ongoing therapy, making the person want more than ever to break negative habits and develop better skills. It can help liberate our clients from therapy blocks due to narrow or limited self-views, as Frank did. This is what happened to Frank, whose therapy really took off once he sensed his SONG OF THE SOUL.

Debra – THE SONG OF THE SOUL

emerging as an afterthought

I hadn't seen Debra for two months, partly because she was in the process of terminating and partly because she was busy with English relatives. Debra had come a long way in therapy. Raised in a small town in England, at first she found our American culture extremely competitive and overwhelming. A very bright and perfectionistic woman, Debra was employed by a major technical company as a high-level technical analyst. She used much of her early therapy to find her bearings, both professionally and in her new environment. As the youngest of a large family, Debra was ill equipped to make many decisions required by a young person living alone in the United States. Eventually, however, she moved in with a young man, a draftsman, whom she planned to marry.

At times Debra had trouble sleeping, often ruminating in the wee hours of the night. Made to feel that she could never get it right growing up, Debra worked overtime in an effort to make sure every-thing was handled with exquisite care. This trait served her well at work, but also promoted a tendency towards isolation by making her more concerned about tasks than with friendships. These issues were all looked at in therapy and she was doing well with them. Now, returning to therapy after her absence of a few months, she declared, "I had a wonderful time with my relatives, I was really able to hold my own with my parents and my brothers and sister. I can see how much easier it is for me to talk to people. I didn't feel terrible way inside anymore when my mother said something."

Of course I responded positively to her news. We discussed a variety of issues and when she said, "I'm really enjoying the new little business that Peter and I have developed," I sensed something new in her. She went on, "It's great. On weekends, we go around to people's homes and organize their attics and basements. You'd be amazed how many people are willing to pay well for this service. I get the chance to work with Peter and we have lots of fun sharing the labor. Peter loves antiques and hooks people up with dealers if they wish. Lots of people really want to get rid of stuff, but don't know how. We even do light chores, such as painting, or cleaning an area, if the people wish. We're so busy that every weekend is full. I have more estimates to go out tomorrow night. I can't believe I finally found a way to have fun with my meticulous nature and earn money, and it's not like my regular job where I have to watch every word. I can wear jeans – we can even look sloppy!'"

Debra had found a way to turn her obsessiveness into something positive. She'd reinvented herself and now had a sense of commitment, joy, connection and purpose. Before my own journey, I might have overlooked her announcement as just an aside because she wasn't bringing up anything that needed my intervention. She was bringing me the resolution! However, I now realized that her information was extremely important in terms not only of validating the work we'd done in therapy, but because she was announcing her own internal capacity to create a way to use for fun and profit a trait that had previously pained her. Debra, too, had found her SONG OF THE SOUL, since her new integration combined commitment, joy and use of special talents.

Sara – a slow emergence of the SONG OF THE SOUL

When Sara was only two, her father died, leaving her mother, an eight year old brother and herself. For years, her mother expressed bitterness and rage at having been left with two small children. Sara was cared for by her grandfather while her mother worked. He, too, was embittered, having come to this country as an immigrant, leaving behind a solid profession which he was never able to work at again. Like Sara's mother, he was punitive, negative and strict. Sara grew up as if under a dark cloud. Her yearning for education and opportunity seemed to bother her family, who ignored her school

149

achievements. Instead of praise for graduating from college, she was put down as the laughing stock of the family for not being married by age twenty-two. Her mother didn't even go to her graduation.

Not surprisingly, as soon as she could earn a living, Sara moved out. Although she succeeded in the business world, her early hurtful family experiences took a toll on her personal relationships. After several relationships failed, she found it hard to trust men, whom she saw as exploitive. In her 30's when she entered therapy, she soon realized that she was a victim of a dysfunctional family and that she was unwittingly reliving some of the behavior that she so hated in them.

After two years of therapy, Sara recognized and acknowledged her talents in a way that was never possible when she lived among her bitter, hostile relatives. She saw that she perceived many people negatively because of the introjects she had absorbed as a child, and she eagerly learned cognitive techniques to help recognize and challenge these stereotypes. She also was able to take risks not possible before therapy. For example, she went on vacation with a girlfriend; she enrolled in a fencing course at the community college; she explored buying a pet. As a result of her research, she decided she wanted to own a parrot. With great care and effort she chose a bird which she felt was right for her. This opened another door, since then she joined a club for parrot owners and joined a pet newsgroup on-line. Gradually her world expanded. She could distance herself from her mother, but still visits to her left her agitated and bitter. As she and her brother talked together and processed their experiences of the family, they developed a much stronger relationship. Sara was invited to participate in his family life and enjoyed being an aunt to his two little children. She also enrolled in a doctoral program in business administration, specializing in computer technology.

One day, Sara came in with the following dream: "I was very angry with my mother who had stolen something of mine. Music played in the background — a song was on the radio. We were sitting at the kitchen table and Mother said to me, 'I don't know why you're so angry at me, you shouldn't be so angry. You're not the only person whose song I've stolen.'"

"I asked Sara what she thought this dream was about. She said she thought the dream meant that she should not take so personally the hurt she experienced from her mother. Indeed, the dream seemed to be saying that her mother had handled many people poorly and Sara just happened to be one of them. We talked about this realization, which I saw as another step in Sara's healing process. Sara's mother had many limitations and certainly was not intentionally trying to hurt her. Sara agreed, saying that, in fact, recently she was able to appreciate the good traits that she'd absorbed or inherited from her mother. For example, as negatively persistent as her mother could be, so Sara can be persistent in positive ways. Even though her mother's persistence sometimes leads to hurt feelings on Sara's part, her own seems to be contributing to her business success.

Going back to Sara's dream, I mentioned how a song seems to be such a personal thing. I shared with her how in my writings I talk about THE SONG OF THE SOUL as a very personal integration of one's own talents, positive memories, capacities and purpose in life, coming from some inner truth. Wouldn't it be a profound violation to have one's "song" stolen in some way? Sara found the concept interesting. We ended the session with my noting that as Sara moved to therapy every other week she seemed to be working well on her own. Perhaps the dream was saying that she still has a Song to be sung that was interrupted by a controlling mother. Perhaps Sara's song is yet to fully emerge. Certainly we wanted to stay alert for it and be ready to welcome it as soon as it came.

After Sara left that night, I found myself in a state of elation. I was excited by having my concept, THE SONG OF THE SOUL, confirmed metaphorically in Sara's dream. Sara's unconscious mind knew how violating it can be when one's song is stolen. When I was developing my concepts, THE SONG OF THE SOUL had floated into my mind as I was looking for terminology to express what was most central to a person's sense of wholeness and authenticity. THE ENCHANTED SELF had also floated in but it did not cover this level of inner harmony. We can feel Enchanted even when all is not harmonic. However, we can only imagine that the ultimate Song of each person's soul would have to be as exquisite as if the angels were singing. I had validation that night that my terminology was on target.

Another night, I asked Sara how she might define her purpose in life, her personal assignment, particularly in light of her background.

Sara immediately replied, "Well I guess I'm one of those people who can shout out, 'The Emperor Has No Clothes.' The truth has always been extremely important to me, even if I have offended someone in attempting to verify it. Sometimes when I was little my mother wouldn't tell us the whole story about why we couldn't do something. For example, she told me I had to make my own clothes in high school. I thought we didn't have enough money for me to buy them. Later I realized it wasn't true. She bought an automobile for cash when I was seventeen. There were many other times over the years when my mother shaded the truth, making me feel more anxious about our money than was necessary or more frightened about various health conditions than was realistic. She shaded the truth to validate her own dark perceptions of the world, e.g., 'People are no good; people let you down; things don't work out; one's body is always a handicap,' and so on. Her distortions made me determined to be a bearer of truth in all situations."

That night, although I was not fully clear about what Sara's SONG OF THE SOUL might be, I had a hunch it would involve the honesty and perseverance of someone who could shout out, "The Emperor Has No Clothes!"

In a recent session, Sara talked about wanting to write a book. She is interested in teaching women, through case studies, she said, how to win the various disputes they often find themselves in, such as dealing with mechanics who overcharge, or with colleagues who disagree. I responded very enthusiastically to Sara's potential book. She could certainly see my face was glowing as I listened to her. I commented that the topic excited me. I thought there would be many people, including men, who would be eager to learn how to get their just desserts in this world. By the end of the session we were both glowing in anticipation of her project. This book would certainly be a wonderful use of Sara's talents. She's bright, she's organized, she's persistent and she's determined to find justice for herself and for others. I realized that Sara would certainly sing her SONG OF THE SOUL as she wrote her book. As her therapist I felt satisfaction that I'd helped Sara get to the place where her SONG OF THE SOUL was beginning to resonate so clearly. I also felt enhanced by knowing her. As I drove home from that session. I felt as if I was basking in her radiance.

Donna

Readers first met Donna in Chapter V. She was the young woman who came to my office depressed and overwhelmed by job commitments and young children. During early sessions I had helped her to connect with some of her talents and potential. After two years of psychotherapy, Donna was doing well. She was no longer depressed; she was thriving professionally; her children were developing nicely; she and her husband were communicating better, too. In therapy she had worked thorough her anger and disappointment toward the family in which she grew up. Although somewhat passive, Donna changed this style through my support for her creativity. Although Donna had many interpersonal skills, at the time she entered therapy her energy was so closed down that she could not get in touch with her own capacities.

One day towards the end of Donna's therapy, she came in reminiscing about some of the hobbies that had interested her parents when she was growing up. What was so different about this session was the perspective she now had on her parents. Rather than focusing on their dysfunction, she now noted their competencies and emotional health. For example, she talked about her mother's tremendous leadership skills. I pointed out that it was possible that her mother's organizational skills have influenced her own work skills as well as her efficiency in running her home well. She agreed, saying that for the first time in years she felt good talking about her mother.

Several weeks prior to termination, Donna mentioned increasing satisfaction in her marriage, even though her husband had disappointed and angered her that week. He had overdrawn their checking account again. His spending addiction went against their marriage vows, which had stressed that each would be open about spending and stay within the bounds of their income. When she discovered the overdrawn account, he wouldn't discuss the issue. This time, Donna stayed connected even though she was disappointed, rather than totally distancing herself as she had in the past. Probably because of her new attitude, her husband agreed to see a financial counselor. Donna was willing to join him, but he wanted to handle it alone. She was pleased by his initiative. In the same week she started taking photographs again and also resumed her violin lessons. She mentioned that this should be fun because her husband was quite a good pianist and they would be able to play duets together. She ended the session by mentioning a wonderful, restorative couple of hours she had spent on her little girl's bed looking out at the moonlight and stars, feeling peaceful. She wrote this poem about it:

"Women of light, Women of hope, Play the strings of life in the dark, Close to my heart, All that the heavens know and try to teach, Finally I am reached."

I reacted joyfully to Donna's poetry as well as to all her good news. In her last session we talked about how her talents had helped her to heal and we talked about her success in handling difficulties in the marriage even when there was more work to be done. We reminisced about her family of origin as well as about issues regarding her children. We reviewed her professional growth. We hugged and she left confidently, with her head held high and with a bounce in her step.

Later, Donna heard of my interest in recording some of my ideas about positive therapy. She called to ask me if I would like her to write down some of her feelings about her therapy with me. This is what she wrote:

"The way I felt about myself, my life and my future the past several months makes it hard to recreate the feelings of despair and confusion that drove me to therapy two years ago. My recollection of that crisis and the therapeutic process are colored by the fact that something amazing happened along the way – something that made me believe that I could hold within myself the strength and vision to lead a worthwhile life. And that what is 'worthwhile' depends much more on who I am and how I am growing than what I once thought I 'should' be. I think it was your determined work with me to help me rediscover positive aspects of myself and redefine them, when necessary. You constantly helped me highlight the positive in my self-concept that I was currently doing nothing to maintain. Of course this took serious work because I had developed a notion of adulthood based on deferred gratification and suppressing most forms of personal expression that came deep out of my childhood. Actually, by the time I came to you in my thirties, I was experiencing the same despair that my mother had in her thirties, forties and fifties. She had assumed that being a dutiful wife and self-fulfillment were mutually exclusive. When I cried uncontrollably minutes before my wedding, I must have felt I was surrendering to a life of self-abdication. No wonder I felt so depressed by the time I came to see you! You helped me recognize that my father's conservative attitudes had emotionally restricted me and suppressed my own sense of the creative and dramatic. Instinctively my life's choices would have included reading, feminist politics, public accomplishments and artistic hobbies. These were all in stark contrast not only to my dad's view of life but to his attitudes toward my mother. I knew how his attitudes and demands locked my mother into a cage but I didn't have the slightest awareness of the parallel effects on me until we talked in therapy.

You constantly encouraged me to have the courage to own for myself my interests and talents, rather than stifle them. I finally was able to take pride in my talents and my creative spirit as well as in my unconventional nature and not denigrate their value because of my father's fear of the unconventional. This took a lot of work and there were many times when you accompanied me as I gingerly crossed that river.

Tonight, what I remember most clearly is how you helped me again and again to pause and reflect on the positive aspects of how I did things. This eventually led me to rebirth many talents and interests from early years that I had done nothing to maintain. I reread my poetry and essays from high school and college; I got out my violin and played the music I knew so well; I got out the photography I took that had excited me before the time when all my photos were of my kids. I bought new books on feminism and I started reading novels again, remembering how much I loved listening to other people's experiences of life. I got serious about career development and found there was a place for me in the company where my creativity could be utilized in significant ways on the job.

I feel as though my definition of myself had stretched but in fact it simply reincorporated in adult form a 'me' that integrates my earliest talents and dispositional inclinations. You helped me practice communicating and to find ways to gather my energies to try new coping skills. You gave me support in setting priorities and working through assumptions that held me back.

I can honestly say that I like who I am. I like myself so much, I don't even mind sounding corny, because it means so much to me. There have been and will be countless times that something reminds me of an experience in your office and my mind will go to that warm cozy place where we talked. Having that makes it easier to leave without scheduling another appointment!" Donna's last few sentences certainly implied that the therapeutic setting had been a safe haven for her.

Donna is a good example of somebody who now lives a gratifying life in which, in its many facets, she sings her SONG OF THE SOUL. From the past she has been able to draw on talents and creative capacities that now permit her to function with purpose and commitment as well as joy – the very definition of THE SONG OF THE SOUL.

Summary

As readers can see, both Sara and Donna were able to achieve a rich singing of THE SONG OF THE SOUL, if each to a very different tune. Sara lived a somewhat reclusive life, Donna was busy with young children and her husband. Their styles were very different, their interests and hobbies and their pasts were unlike. Yet each was able to retrieve a positive sense of herself. Each experienced the integration that comes with growth in self-esteem and with being able to meet one's needs by weeding through negative past experiences and the messages based on them, to reach positive childhood memories in which they could recognize core interests based on lifelong preferences.

Whereas THE ENCHANTED SELF is a capacity to reclaim and reintegrate positive ego states from the past into joyful ego states in the present, THE SONG OF THE SOUL has the sense of a mission or personal assignment. For Sara, her SONG OF THE SOUL was connected with her mission to yell out "The Emperor Has No Clothes." Donna's SONG OF THE SOUL was multi-dimensional, utilizing her creativity and talents in many areas of her life.

As I mentioned earlier in this chapter, most of our clients will leave therapy without singing their full SONG OF THE SOUL. But as all therapists know, some of the benefits of psychotherapy may flower many years later. THE ENCHANTED SELF therapist gives the training that will lead to the recognition and naming of her client's most positive qualities, along with encouragement to realize their fullest expression in her life, whenever that might be. To help a client identify and integrate her SONG OF THE SOUL, the clinician needs to:

1. Promote self regard
2. Provide techniques the client can use to get her needs met
3. Teach her how to recognize and retrieve earlier positive states of being
4. Teach her how to transfer learning from a successful area of life to a less successful area.

Reader's exercise

1. If you feel you already have a sense of your SONG OF THE SOUL, take some pleasure in thinking about it. Try to put into words, or into other forms of expression (such as drawing or movement), what you think your SONG OF THE SOUL is.

2. If you are not aware of your SONG OF THE SOUL, write down five positive aspects or attributes of yourself that reflect your strengths, preferences, talents, or potential. Look at your list and let your mind wander. Jot down some possible ways they could combine to form your SONG OF THE SOUL.

3. Stay alert over the next six months for aspects of yourself that are special and unique, and where you feel such a commitment, intensity, or passion that they may well belong to your SONG OF THE SOUL. My hope is that through reading this material you will have the courage to name, validate and celebrate your special talents. Perhaps you will unveil a special commitment or a sense of an assignment in life as you think about yourself, that you have not previously taken the time to recognize or applaud.

For example one might reflect upon the following talents and traits in oneself: artistic, good tennis player, charitable, loves children.

Perhaps this person could see her SONG OF THE SOUL developing as a recreational counselor, or as a volunteer teaching children certain sports, including tennis. Or, maybe these particular characteristics would sing by giving children, grandchildren, or even a friend's child, opportunities not only to learn how to play tennis but to appreciate art.

Thus, I am asking you to play with combinations of your talents, preferences, potentials and strengths in new ways – ways that incorporate within them a sense of purpose and commitment, as well as realistically being able to fit into your life.

Chapter Eleven

Using THE ENCHANTED SELF

THE ENCHANTED SELF as a mosaic

Dorothy

Dorothy came into my office, saying eagerly, "I think I figured out a way to use THE ENCHANTED SELF. I'm thinking of THE ENCHANTED SELF as a mosaic. When you asked me to find Enchanted Moments from earlier days," (*What I have taught in this book as Positive Fingerprints or Positive Shadowprints of the Mind*) "I had no trouble coming up with some beautiful images. I can see myself in a glorious field, when I was eight, chasing butterflies. I can see myself at eleven walking downtown with my friend, delighting in each other's companionship, thrilled to be buying some little notions together at the "Five and Dime." However, when I would try to bring these images forward and see how I could use them now, I felt blocked. Immediately my head filled with negative messages, like, 'You don't deserve that!' 'That was just one moment in time.' 'You don't have the time for such luxuries.' 'What do you expect to accomplish?' 'Who do you think you are?'

But the other day the notion of a mosaic just floated into my head. It, too, goes with a positive memory from an Enchanted Moment in the past — when my grandmother took me to the Art Institute in Philadelphia when I was a little girl. We wandered around from room to room and looked at the mummies and the Impressionists and I remember being intrigued by the mosaics. How had they made those beautiful pictures out of fragments? It was that image that helped me because I suddenly saw all my past Enchanted Moments as mosaic fragments of potential. They were in different shapes — some were oddly shaped, some beautifully shaped. They were of different colors, some were dark, some were light. Each one could be moved around like you can do with a mosaic and each could become part of a new configuration. Each was in a shape that in and of itself might look odd or funny or misshapen but might be the perfect shape to finish an angle in a current pattern. Similarly, the shape that seemed dark might be moved in such a way as to provide lightness in another design. Somehow this image of THE ENCHANTED SELF as a mosaic began to get me around some sort of obstacle."

We went on processing the mosaic image. I commented that it seemed to be a very exciting idea because so many people suffer from negative story lines that surround Enchanted Moments, both while experiencing the moment and in the thread that links that moment to the rest of their lives. Taking the moment out, metaphorically speaking, and placing it elsewhere as a piece of mosaic, frees it. It can belong uniquely to the individual because it is her memory, but it doesn't stay enmeshed in the dysfunctional aspects of her history. Even a moment that was not truly glorious, even a "dark moment" may have had within it elements of that person's talents, strengths, potential and preferences. Again by taking it out and separating it as only a chip on a mosaic, the darkness can lose its contaminating quality. In a new position that chip can fit into a new mosaic in just the right way to help the person find her ENCHANTED SELF.

As we played back and forth with this image, Dorothy decided that she wanted to take three or four of her Enchanted Moments from childhood and, in a fashion, reconfigure them. For example, she had collected glass and stones as a child and still had some of her own, as well as her mother's collection. She wanted to make these collections alive again. She said this would help her bring her mosaic chips forward from her childhood. She hadn't gone down the whole road yet, but had the mosaic image and wanted to play with it. I encouraged her to do so, mentioning to Dorothy that she might want to look for chips from her past that were more abstract than seaglass and stones. I thought some of the chips might be such things as her imagination and her creativity. And these, too, might come alive and be able to flower now that they were disconnected from negative messages. Dorothy agreed, saying that this was the first time in many years that she could feel her creativity actually flow! She, noted, "I often say to my friends, 'I have a muse but she is off sleeping'." I responded to Dorothy that it was exciting that this part of her came back. With reassurance and support, instead of criticism, perhaps it would take root and grow.

The 'mosaic' session was an inspirational session for both Dorothy and myself. For Dorothy, it revealed a new way to explore and look for positive aspects of herself without the interference of internalized dysfunctional thoughts. Even though fascinated by THE ENCHANTED SELF concept, she'd previously been unable to find a way to use it beyond the memory of an Enchanted Moment. Suddenly, she managed to find an unique way to reframe parts of her past so that they become useful to her and in doing so, she stretched the concept of "reframing" beyond how I perceived it and indeed, she did "reframe." My own vision had been expanded and enlightened, as so often we therapists find it is in our work.

For many people, "reframing" as I use the term, works, with the therapist's help and the client's capacities to find the silver lining in their own stories. In retelling one's story so that certain positive aspects are emphasized and negative ones de-emphasized or deleted, the individual has a new chance to define who one is and to become aware of previously hidden talents and potential. However, for many people with extremely dysfunctional backgrounds, there is so much pain. It's too hard to know how to move away from deeply entrenched, negative internalized scripts about oneself, to a fresh start and a new way of seeing oneself. Utilizing the mosaic may be one alternative.

THE ENCHANTED SELF concept is far from complete. As a technique and a paradigm it's still in the developmental stages. Through this book you have been exposed to several ways to use the concept. Many clients (as well as yourself) may respond to THE ENCHANTED SELF and even be able to sing the SONG OF THE SOUL. The approaches mentioned in this book, including renaming, reframing, sorting out the functional from the dysfunctional, learning how to identify Positive Fingerprints and Positive Shadowprints of the Mind, improving one's self-esteem and learning how to get one's needs met, can help everyone achieve better mental health as we find unexpected sources of strength and happiness in our ENCHANTED SELVES.

THE ENCHANTED SELF in the
treatment room

I intentionally started this summary chapter with Dorothy's approach to give you a sense, as we draw to a close, of how unique this model is. It allows the therapist to encourage in both traditional and creative ways what is functional, rather than dysfunctional, about your client. It gives you and the client a way to highlight those positive aspects of herself while still practicing your chosen form of psychotherapy.

How does ENCHANTED SELF therapy differ from other forms of psychotherapy? It's different because it emphasizes the positive. Imagine that ENCHANTED SELF therapy is a lens that when placed over another technique, magnifies and sharpens the positive aspects of the client's history and personality. Looking at one's clients this way one sees them as survivors and as talented, wondrous people. In order to help them appreciate their talents, the therapist asks questions and looks for answers in ways that enhance the individual, rather them focusing strictly on the present "problem" or clearly dysfunctional aspects of the person's life. In this way it can be readily used with many modalities, including insight-oriented therapy, family systems therapy, cognitive therapy, behavioral therapy, Gestalt Therapy, Feminist Therapy and others. I have used it successfully with individuals, couples and families.

THE ENCHANTED SELF as a paradigm shift

THE ENCHANTED SELF is always an attitudinal shift on the part of the therapist in the treatment room in her relationship to the client, as well as her handling of the therapeutic hour.

THE ENCHANTED SELF lens

The following is a summary of these shifts:

1. As the therapist, one is on the alert for ways to reinforce what is "good news" about one's client, happy memories and information that indicates potential talents, strengths or capacities. This is a general stance, an attitude. It becomes a direct technique when appropriate.

2. When the client shares negative information about herself, no matter how valid this information may be, the therapist makes an attempt to give feedback with reference to the client's talents, capacities, strengths and/or potential. This simple technique permits the therapist to frame inadequacies in such a way that the client can still perceive her potential. This stance emphasizes the therapist's positive regard for her client.

3. If negative information about the person does not lend itself in any fashion to positive feedback and if there is no honest way that the therapist can reinforce talents or potential, she still maintains that there is more that is positive and workable within the person than is coming through at this time. The therapist doesn't allow her client to feel that this negative information is seen as global, but rather as merely partial.

4. The therapist teaches clients how to look for positive news about themselves and how to practice the art of positive thinking. The therapist teaches her clients how to recognize positive states of mind and provides techniques for developing positive thinking, thus encouraging positive states of mind.

THE ENCHANTED SELF as a modality can include specific approaches, mentioned in earlier chapters. These approaches include

1. Helping the client sort and separate functional aspects of her past from dysfunctional.
2. Helping the client rename and reframe aspects of her past in order to recognize what was positive.
3. Helping the client to recognize Fingerprints of the Mind and Positive Shadowprints of the Mind.
4. Helping the client to improve her self-esteem.
5. Teaching the client techniques for getting her needs met.

163

Pacing therapy

Because ENCHANTED SELF therapy emphasizes the client's strengths and talents rather than weaknesses, as affirmed by the therapist, progress can be rapid, particularly for clients who don't exhibit severe pathology. Affirming the client's capacities for survival and helping her explore untapped potential may shorten therapy time, especially if she enters therapy with anxiety and depression generated or heightened by current life circumstances.

Couples and families, too, benefit from hearing more good news about themselves than they usually hear in traditional therapy. Resilience to conflicts and negative messages from intimates may be strengthened by ENCHANTED SELF therapy. For many years therapists have been trained to acknowledge and confirm the "bad news" clients bring, perceiving "bad news" as reflective of long standing patterns. I'm suggesting that we therapists assume that clients have more need to "work through" issues than may be necessary. For many people a safe holding environment that contains within it a respectful, reciprocal relationship where the "professional" recognizes "good news" and teaches the client how to retrieve, recognize and use her talents, strengths, preferences and potential, may facilitate a quicker recovery as optimism returns. Positive energies are contagious just as negative ones are.

I do not see THE ENCHANTED SELF as encouraging abuse of legitimate psychotherapy goals which could easily happen in American mental health today, with the pressures on therapists to move toward short term treatment. I would not like to see my ENCHANTED SELF therapy used to curtail or shorten psychotherapy, just to save money for insurance companies, when this may compromise treatment. Then, too, occasionally, as in any encounter with a client, material in THE ENCHANTED SELF therapy may emerge that the therapist is not prepared for. When this material emerges, be it a history of violence or abuse or perhaps more serious pathology, the therapist must go with what has emerged and use all her clinical skills to offer the best possible treatment. On those occasions, therapy may be heading for a much longer commitment.

THE ENCHANTED SELF therapy is not intended as a short-cut or a way to trivialize the intricacies of the human mind. Rather,

164

it is a method of establishing more hope and optimism in both the client and therapist sooner and more effectively than through other modalities.

Cautions

THE ENCHANTED SELF therapy works well with many conditions, including anxiety, mild to moderate depression and immaturity. People in life transitions, those dealing with acute traumas, physical illness, loss of a significant person, work stress and inferiority feelings are all solid candidates for THE ENCHANTED SELF therapy. However there are certain instances where a therapist may find that THE ENCHANTED SELF therapy may not be effective. These may include:

1. PSYCHOSIS. Those clients who suddenly or chronically present psychotic processing such as delusions, hallucinations, or other thought disorders that keep them from staying consistently oriented are not likely to benefit from THE ENCHANTED SELF therapy, although they may from parts of it. For example, although a psychotic client may spend some time in a hospital and may very likely be medicated by another professional, you, as primary therapist, may still find many opportunities to point out the client's strengths either to the client when she is oriented and able to accept positive information, or to family members who may also be involved in the therapy.

2. SEVERE (AND PSYCHOTIC) DEPRESSION. If your client presents major depressive symptomatology, as outlined in the DSM III or IV,[21] it would be inappropriate to focus on THE ENCHANTED SELF until depressive symptoms have been alleviated and there is no danger of suicide. But once this has occurred, looking for and pointing out positive aspects of the client to her or to her family members can be very helpful. The key is whether the client is yet able to hear and accept good news. This requires sensitive timing and testing of the waters. A depressed client may think the therapist is not paying attention to her or feeling her pain if the therapist dwells too much on the positive. One can assume, however, that if the therapist is seeing the client for long term therapy she may certainly find an opportunity in the recovery process to teach

her how to recognize and utilize positive states of mind and how to get her needs met and improve her self-esteem.

3. ADDICTIONS. THE ENCHANTED SELF therapy is not your first line of attack with an addicted client. The addiction needs to be curbed and for that there are specific treatment modalities. Once the client has her addictive behavior under control and is ready to pursue her growth at the insight level, THE ENCHANTED SELF approaches to treatment should assist you.

4. DISASSOCIATIVE STATES – INCLUDING MULTIPLE PERSONALITIES. Again, as with addictive behaviors, there are specialized treatment modalities for dissociative states, such as trance and hypnotic approaches. THE ENCHANTED SELF therapy may be used at times, allowing the therapist to maintain positive regard toward the client, while looking for ways to recognize and acknowledge good news about the client when appropriate.

Remaining realistic – the WAVE EFFECT when using THE ENCHANTED SELF approach

The WAVE EFFECT is the way we grow and change in an undulating rhythm. We go forward, backward and then again forward and backward, like the waves coming in to shore. Sometimes improvement is all but imperceptible. Imagine sitting in a low beach chair on the shore. Each wave seems to hit us between our ankles and our knees. Suddenly a wave comes in higher. Now we are wet from head to toe. Similarly in life, both our clients and ourselves grow in such a way that we are not always aware of or prepared for the changes. As we practice THE ENCHANTED SELF technique both with our clients and with ourselves, we may feel disappointed if progress isn't consistent. This disappointment may be particularly difficult to process now that we have taken the giant step forward of seeing both our clients and ourselves in a much more positive light. If we do not think too highly of someone, it is often easier to accept their shortcomings than if we truly admire someone. Now that each and every client may have become a heroine or a hero for us, as we maintain a positive stance and attitude toward him or her, we may feel defeated when the client shows up and tells us that her spouse stepped all over her again or that she was unable to go to the new job after accepting it, or that she felt totally broken inside having heard some negative feedback from someone close to her. But, realizing that the WAVE EFFECT in just as common in THE ENCHANTED SELF therapy as it is in all growth, one can relax and go with it.

To conclude, when used in a timely manner, THE ENCHANTED SELF is restorative to both the client and to the therapist. The client benefits from being taught how to look for good news within herself, how to get her needs met and how to improve her self-esteem. At the same time she works on her genuine therapeutic issues. She benefits from a holding environment which provides a reciprocal relationship with her therapist – one in which the therapist is not a blank wall but a caring person willing to teach, support, validate and encourage the client in many different ways. The therapist benefits because she can experience the flow, enjoying the reciprocal nature of the treatment hour. Viewing her clients in a positive light as wonderful people who are survivors with untapped potential, dreams and talents, heightens the pleasure of her time with her clients. Rather than experiencing some of the energy drain that happens when one is always on a search and discovery mission for bad news, she can participate in the search for what's good – what could work for the client and what may have worked in the past. The positive aspects of the client are always being emphasized. Even when the therapist must still point out painful and difficult material, she can gain strength from having found a way to share such news in such a fashion as not to break someone down but to build them up. This type of therapeutic relationship assists the therapist in moving away from the somewhat depressive position that many therapists find themselves in chronically, and it can help them avoid complete burn-out and exhaustion.

In practicing the art of positive retrieval with her clients, the therapist will begin to recognize talents and potential within herself. She will find herself enjoying many opportunities to learn from her clients, who will often share wonderful treasure troves of talents, information and skills as they flower. As the therapist you will have the opportunity to see each client as a wondrous human spirit. You will often find yourself able to help your client recognize the private heroine within, rather than just helping her to feel or function better. Inside of each client there is someone who yearns to be liberated from distortions and dysfunctional patterns. Within your client, as within yourself, is a spirit that is creative and emotionally healthy and as full of energy as those qualities imply.

This is where I come back to the full circle of THE ENCHANTED SELF concept. The more you become your own hero or heroine, the more you, too, can break free from your dysfunctional past – and be able to acknowledge, recognize and understand your own talents, strengths and potential. Your own journey will give you more compassion for others as well as a way to understand your own inner processing as you support your clients on their journeys.

I am talking about the power of habits and in this case, positive mental habits, as well as the power of reciprocal learning. The more often you reach back into your own past and retrieve positive memories and the more often you use these memories to weave themselves into the fabric of your current self, the more habitual this process becomes. It feels like coming home. You have now practiced reconnection with the positive earlier aspects of yourself again and again until they flash out, 'I'M YOUR ENCHANTED SELF, TAKE ME, BRING ME FORWARD, USE ME, LOVE ME' again and again. And the more that you see parts of your current self as having positive energy that links you to your own memory bank, the more you'll bring excitement and hope into your therapy room, teaching and sharing a process that has already become habitual and enriching for you, personally.

In Chapter XII, we'll look again at my personal journey. I want to share with you my SONG OF THE SOUL as I currently live it.

Chapter Twelve

Coming Full Circle Singing My SONG OF THE SOUL

YOU notice that everything an Indian does is in a circle and this is because the power of the world always works in circles and everything tries to be round.[22]

THE ENCHANTED SELF I

> Come to me –
> innocent that I was,
> I'll join you and together
> We'll melt into the new dawn of me.
>
> Come my friend,
> my nurturer, my shadow –
> My knowledge of how whole I can be!
>
> Barbara

As I've noted, our clients don't come into our offices feeling like heroes and heroines. Instead, they come in feeling like broken people living lives of despair. It becomes our job and challenge to help them rediscover and use their strengths. In the previous chapters, I taught

169

you how to separate out from one's dysfunctional past (be it your client's or your own), positive aspects of one's self. I shared with you techniques such as renaming and reframing that facilitate selecting and recognizing positive memories. We learned about different types of memories, cognitive and affective, as well as memories of real events and memories of dreams and fantasies. After studying these Positive Fingerprints and Shadowprints of the Mind, we discussed THE ENCHANTED SELF as a multi-dimensional, positive state of being, experienced when there is sufficient self-esteem, when one's needs have been adequately met, and when one has recognized and exercised one's strengths. Finally, I shared with you some of the culminating effects of this process, particularly THE SONG OF THE SOUL. Although some people may sing their SONG OF THE SOUL in all spheres of their lives, others may sing it only in one. Yet, whenever one sings it, one experiences not just an ENCHANTED MOMENT or THE ENCHANTED SELF, but rather feels touched by meaning and purpose to the very core. And although a person may sing her SONG OF THE SOUL many different ways over a lifetime, she'll be aware of a thread of continuity that ties into her unique essence.

Each chapter has ended with exercises, giving you the opportunity to begin to process and better understand your own Enchantment. In Chapter IV, I talked about my SONG OF THE SOUL. Now I would like to finish telling you my story up to this point in time.

As you read in Chapter IV, by not naming myself properly, I could not value or validate what was most Enchanting about myself. This mislabeling of talents, strengths and preferences had put me into conflict. I had trouble enjoying my talents with a pure heart, as I was in conflict over my identification with my father. I could not permit myself to value myself for "masculine" traits or talents. Yet I had no adequate way to relabel them so that I could feel whole. I wanted to be "womanly," but many of my earlier experiences had left me filled with a sense of female weakness and inadequacy. I loved my mother dearly, yet because of my family's dysfunction and the messages I received from them about women, I couldn't find a way to fully incorporate all of my talents, preferences and interests into a "feminine" identity that I could accept.

I was left unable to know how to label what I wanted to bring forth as most competent, most wonderful and most central about myself. If I had brought forth all of the things my father had taught me and left them labeled as "masculine," I would have thrown myself into conflict about identifying with "masculine" traits. If I had attempted to bring forth what I thought was feminine from my childhood, these images were so laden with despair and failure that I would have been courting depression. In an effort to accommodate, I did bring forth many talents that my father had encouraged in me and that I had identified with in him. This allowed me to achieve professionally. But the true joy of feeling totally at ease with oneself, having comfortably named oneself, was denied to me because of my family of origin's negative attitudes. I yearned to be powerful, I yearned to be a caretaker, I yearned to be loved and be lovable and yet, I didn't know what to call myself.

And so, I felt an emptiness as a mature professional woman in our society. I experienced the fragmentation of our current society, at the same time as I experienced the "one down" position felt by so many women. I felt overwhelmed by the competitive aspects of our society and the pressure for public recognition. I missed any validation for the private moment or the private happening. My various therapies had healed me significantly, but I still lacked a sense of myself as personally whole and valuable to society at the same time. As I've mentioned, there were many steps along the way that helped me feel more con- nected to my feminine side as well as finally finding a satisfactory defi- nition of womanhood that incorporated the traits I considered to be positive. The core definition that worked for me was the Judaic concept of the "wise women." As I studied with my Torah teacher and gained a deep comprehension of the Biblical woman as wise and courageous, as spiritual at the deepest level, I found myself feeling healed. I felt that all my positive talents and perceptions finally had a home.

Only as I was able to understand the real essence of the feminine in broader and broader terms, taking me to the most current feminist literature, as well as the oldest biblical references, was I able to find, retrieve and be my ENCHANTED SELF. It was profoundly moving to me to learn in my Judaic studies that Biblical women were valued as highly spiritual beings and as significant agents of change through their courage and sensitive natures. I knew I was one of their true descendants.

From that time, my life took on powerful meaning. One of Judaism's concepts is that nothing happens for naught. Every experience teaches

171

you and better equips you for your assignment in life. Each person has a unique purpose. Viewing my life this way gave me optimism and hope about my past that I had never had before. The bleak dark days of childhood and even my early adult years, so lacking in the harmony I often wished for, had, I could now see, been of service to me. The pain that I felt and the less than fulfilling time I'd spent, had all prepared me to better appreciate my wholeness and made sense in my determination to be in the service of others. Yet, it wasn't easy.

A personal reflection

I want to share an experience from a few years ago. I was on a train going to New York for a day's outing with a very dear friend. She asked as we chatted, "Whatever happened to those interviews you did with women? You seemed so excited about what you had discovered."

I answered, "Well, I did write a couple of articles and I wrote some chapters for a book about the women. I even sent them out to some agents, but they were rejected. I can better understand why, now that I have further conceptualized my theory of THE ENCHANTED SELF. However, it did deflate me. Then I seemed to get so involved with other things: our son's Bar Mitzvah; our parents were getting older; our daughter was finishing college and ..." I found myself going on and on listing reasons, or I should say excuses. Suddenly, I said to her, "If I don't write the book on THE ENCHANTED SELF, then I'm not only letting myself down, but I'm letting down the people who've shared themselves with me. The positive news about people that I was able to learn from them will never be communicated beyond me." My friend agreed and encouraged me to get back to my writing.

More time passed. It took major surgery, a recovery and many other growth experiences along the way for me to develop enough sense of self to put limits around my time and space and defend my privacy, so that I could get to the pages that you are now reading. I had to alter my expectations and shift gears.

This is what I did: I kept my practice smaller even after I'd fully recovered from my surgery. However, the raft shook. My income was lower, my priorities were different, and my self-perceptions had shifted. I no longer saw myself as primarily a therapist. I was also a communicator and a seeker. While new to my adult life, these represented earlier commitments that I had left behind. On the raft were my husband, our children, our parents and many other significant people. I had to redefine myself to each of them. Each redefinition strengthened me ultimately, but in the short run sometimes resulted in anxiety and guilt as we all struggled to keep the raft afloat. Whenever I felt these painful emotions I practiced the art of positive thinking, just the way I suggest that my clients do. Writing about my research with women and my new clinical theories has helped me to reinforce positive "self" messages.

My own SONG OF THE SOUL comes through in several different harmonies. I'm not sure that it crosses every area of my life but I'm sure that it intersects my professional life because I feel tremendously dedicated to making a correction in the psychological literature toward the positive. I believe I have the understanding and background to help others see that we need to think more positively about our personal histories and in the way we envision ourselves and others. I have the opportunity to do this with my clients, as well as to write about it – to help get the word out.

I am more than a practicing psychologist in the treatment room. I'm an artist who writes poetry and prose, who acts and who is creative in many other ways. I am also the frustrated dancer who was told she would be too tall.

This brings me to another facet of my SONG OF THE SOUL that I want to share with you. One of the healers who helped me with hands on restorative work after my hysterectomy was Doreen Laperdon-Addison, a Movement Educator and Choreographer. We'd met and befriended each other in ballet class. When the surgery took place, she came over to my house and did some bodywork with me in those first couple of months.

As I recovered I talked to her about my ENCHANTED SELF concepts. She was intrigued and asked to read my material. I'd written several articles, based on my initial case studies, which I'd presented at conferences, and I had the unpublished book chapters on my initial research. Doreen came back excited, having read the material, and we brainstormed. We came up with a notion of THE ENCHANTED SELF Mind/Body Workshops that would help the public come in touch with positive aspects of their minds and bodies. She also wished to choreograph a dance entitled THE ENCHANTED SELF. I was so awed and elated when Doreen said she would like to choreograph this dance! I could hardly believe that she thought my concept valuable enough to turn into an art form – or that she valued me enough to give me a part in the performance. When, finally, a twenty-three minute dance emerged, I was amazed.

I danced the part of the Enchantress, the woman who, metaphorically, transmitted THE ENCHANTED SELF. I was passing the good news down from one generation to another in an endless learning circle. Dancing in this professional production was a culminating moment in my life. Considering many of the negative messages I, too, struggle with, the dance represented for me overcoming the dark side of many of my internalized messages, particularly around my body image. (see photographs below)

I Excerpt from
THE ENCHANTED SELF DANCE, BARBARA
photos by Emily Doherty

II Excerpt from
THE ENCHANTED SELF
DANCE, BARBARA,
BRIANNE

III Excerpt from
THE ENCHANTED SELF DANCE,
BARBARA, DOREEN AND BRIANNE
photos by Emily Doherty

V Excerpt from
THE ENCHANTED SELF
DANCE, BARBARA, DOREEN

IV Excerpt from
THE ENCHANTED SELF DANCE,
DOREEN

175

Doreen and I worked on conceptualizing the Mind/Body Workshops for a year before we began running them. Since then, we have presented THE ENCHANTED SELF Mind/Body Workshops in many settings, including schools, senior citizen centers, clubs, women's meetings, and at conferences for mental health professionals. The dance was presented twice, the second time in the Spring of 1994 at Brookdale Community College as the "opener" for The Women's Voices Journey of Discovery Day. Three hundred women saw the dance and forty-five participated in THE ENCHANTED SELF Mind/Body Workshop.

The Mind/Body Workshops taught us that everyone needs replenishment. People of all ages and backgrounds enjoy retrieving their unique and personal positive memories through cognitive and physical activities. The mental health professionals who have attended the workshops have shown a clear need for replenishment and have welcomed ways to value themselves more than they do. Together we have written an article that summarizes how THE ENCHANTED SELF Mind/Shop Workshops affected mental health Professionals.[23]

Working with Doreen and collaborating on THE ENCHANTED SELF Mind/Body workshops has forced me to activate many talents and capacities that are different from those I bring to the therapy room or to my writing. I've been stretched and pulled in new ways that are at the same time a return to old childhood talents such as acting, showmanship and giving oral presentations. Sharing processing and decision making in forming and carrying out the workshops stretched me beyond childhood experiences, letting me finally execute unrealized dreams and potential. Having grown up as an only child until I was seventeen, when my sister Diane was born, I often felt lonely and without enough companions to cheer me on. I used to imagine myself with a friend or friends putting on plays and writing stories together. Now I'm living it!

Unlike the therapy room, the workshops give me an opportunity for immediate feedback from strangers concerning THE ENCHANTED SELF as a concept as well as a technique. This has been extremely helpful in developing THE ENCHANTED SELF. Obviously in long-term individual therapy, the client's needs take precedence over the therapist's desire for feedback.

In the spring of 1995, Doreen Laperdon-Addison and I started THE ENCHANTED SELF NEWSLETTER. This newsletter provides a forum to reach out to others so that they can share their good news about themselves. It gives us an opportunity to teach THE ENCHANTED SELF to the public while giving readers a vehicle for sharing their good news and talking to each other. This newsletter is another effort to offset negativity in our society by teaching people how to recognize and share their talents, their potential and their enhanced moments.

As I look at my past, all of my strengths, both those appreciated and those ignored when I was growing up, are now employed in one forum or another through my personal assignment, which is to create and communicate THE ENCHANTED SELF concept. I am a listener, a teacher, a communicator, a student. I am a poetess, a performer, a dancer, I am a holder of wise knowledge. I am a healer. I can come through!

Perhaps this little poem says something of my sense of personal awakening:

THE ENCHANTED SELF II

> *Devalued when born*
> *Fed but not nourished*
> *Asleep but not dead*
> *Sleeping beauty – awakened! Beautiful woman*
> *Beautiful soul –*
> *Beautiful person!*
>
> Barbara

THE ENCHANTED SELF

My hope and dream is that you as the clinician will thrust yourself back into the treatment room helping your clients to get in touch with their ENCHANTED SELF.

My hope and dream is also that you as the reader, whoever you are, will thrust yourself back into the world with a determination to get further in touch with your ENCHANTED SELF. I believe I've shared enough of myself and my clients to give you courage to start this journey. If you determine that you need therapy in order to go on your journey, whether you are a clinician, an allied professional, or a "lay person," I encourage you to persevere in finding a therapist who is able to help you bring out your most positive aspects of yourself so that you can mobilize them toward your goals. Courageously interview a potential therapist just as she will interview you. Look for someone who interacts with you in a reciprocal way that helps you feel comfortable. Look for someone who does not dwell on negative information but seems interested in emphasizing your positive traits, strengths and talents. Look for someone who can make you feel you're in a safe holding environment, valued for who you are. Ask the therapist what her philosophy is about human nature and the potential for growth.

If you choose to pursue and continue your ENCHANTED SELF journey by yourself, I hope you will talk about it with others and find ways to be in reciprocal relationships, sharing positive aspects of yourself, as well as documenting and validating for others their positive capacities. Don't keep your journey a secret. Remember, your ENCHANTED SELF is not out there in some Enchanted Forest in Fantasyland, but is already a part of yourself waiting to be reclaimed and truly valued.

I wish you a joyful journey. I hope that your life feels whole and that you find in your past, whether beautiful or painful, a repertoire of talents and capacities that are uniquely yours. I hope that your talents, capacities and potential will give you a sense of well-being as they thrust you into the world in meaningful ways.

Conclusion

I have a very deep desire to know how we affect each other in positive ways. Please write to me and share your efforts. As a clinician, how have your clients responded to THE ENCHANTED SELF techniques? What has worked? What hasn't worked? Can you share some of their narratives? To the reader in general, I also ask for your responses. Were you able to retrieve positive information about yourself as well as integrate your positive memories into new capacities for enhanced living? Let me know some of your ENCHANTED

MOMENTS. Tell me if you find yourself able to live your ENCHANTED SELF at least some of the time. Let me know if you think you have discovered your SONG OF YOUR SOUL. Let me know if a particular exercise worked for you at the end of a chapter. Let me know if the book needed to emphasize more clearly a particular point or to develop a section more extensively. THE ENCHANTED SELF is an evolving concept and you may have important feedback. Your personal comments, responses and anecdotal information can help in the process of further developing THE ENCHANTED SELF concept.[21]

Please write to the following address:

THE ENCHANTED SELF
P.O. Box 2112
Ocean, NJ 07712

If you would like to receive THE ENCHANTED SELF newsletter write to the above address.

If you wish to communicate directly with me via the World Wide Web, look for THE ENCHANTED SELF home page at http://www.enchantedself.com/ or write to me at ENCSELF@ aol.com.

A blessing

I am changed by you Forever
Let it be good!
Let my influence on you be life-enhancing and yours on mine
May we learn from each other, golden threads of selfhood and together may
    we make a life-enhancing tapestry
Let me always remember that the teacher is in the student
 And, in awe, I see the beauty in all.

Barbara

The End

Enchanted Self by Peter Eno

"Cant N. hence Adj. and V.
Whence canter and canting,
The singing,
Whining utterance
    of certain preachers
(and from much earlier)
    of beggars.

To sing or chant
L (latin) cantus, cantare …
Cantata …
Becomes OF (old French) chanter
    to chant.★

Enchantment:
In singing, in song.

Wrapped in the power of a spell
Cast by words or a song, something you said or a sound,

Did I remember it? Something precious!
Or did I forget for a moment all the worries I carry around?

Self: from old English, old German
Norwegian, old Danish, and Irish
And finally perhaps Old Celtic
From Selva: possession.

Possess: from latin is 'potis'
To be master of,
To make oneself master of.

Therefore:
The enchanted self,
Master of remembering
The song of myself,
rapt in joy, and wonder of wonders★★
I remember the love.

★Eric Partridge: Origins
★★On Buddha's awakening he exclaimed, "Wonder of wonders, all
beings have this same inherent enlightened mind!

Glossary

Definitions of ENCHANTED SELF Concepts

1. THE ENCHANTED SELF As used in this book refers to positive states of being, as well as the Paradigm Shift in the Treatment Room as defined below.

THE ENCHANTED SELF as a state of being is the person's capacity to incorporate within them unique positive aspects qualities recombined in such way as to provide a positive experience in the present. THE ENCHANTED SELF does assume some degree of continuity and the capacity of the person to self-generate this positive state of being. Because it is internally generated there is the assumption that the person has appropriate self-esteem and knowledge of how to have her needs met at least so far as experiencing this positive state of being. These two components may not be necessary to experience the Enchanted Moment.

THE ENCHANTED SELF as a Paradigm Shift in the Treatment Room: The therapist looks at her clients through different lenses, seeing them as survivors and as talented wondrous people who come into therapy with problems or disorders. In order to assist them in the appreciation of their talents she asks questions and looks for answers in ways that enhance the person rather than focusing strictly on the presented "problem" or clearly dysfunctional aspects of the person's life.

Certain assumption are now made by the therapist, including a sense of mutuality with the client at all times, a positive regard for the client, a perceptual shift so that the client is always perceived as a survivor, i.e., a heroine in the making rather then a dysfunctional person. The therapist is an active teacher of positive thinking who helps the client learn how to perceive herself in a more positive fashion.

2. POSITIVE FINGERPRINTS OF THE MIND: These are conscious memories containing positive material that was lived or imagined by the person. The material is unique to the individual.

3. POSITIVE SHADOWPRINTS OF THE MIND: These are sensations and/or other forms of subtle memories that contain within them experienced or imagined positive happenings that are unique to that individual.

Both Positive Fingerprints and Shadowprints of the Mind may contain positive images, devalued or not recognized by the client, or they may contain both positive and negative components. This is where the therapist's work in helping the client to rename and re-frame her personal information becomes critical.

4. POSITIVE FINGERPRINTS OF THE BODY: These are positive memories that can be retrieved through the body. Once retrieved they can be utilized to help the person achieve positive states of being more often. For example, if somebody can get in touch with a sensation of rocking or swaying from side to side that feels pleasurable and restorative, then repetition and or reintegration of that movement can be encouraged in positive ways. Thus the person can learn to relax by utilizing these movements as she listens to her favorite music. Or there may be ways to incorporate these movements into sport or hobby. Rocking may lend itself to learning to row a boat. Swaying may lend itself to dance.

For further information on the concept of how Enchanted states of well being can be encouraged via Positive Fingerprints of the Body, see the article, "GROUP WORK For Mental Health Providers Utilizing THE ENCHANTED SELF CONCEPT."

5. THE ENCHANTED MOMENT: The Enchanted Moment is when a person is able to experience a joyful state of being that incorporates some of her uniqueness. The Enchanted Moment can be inspired or generated by external forces such as a workshop or a

184

seminar or even by reading a good novel. The very word "moment"connotes that there is no certainty that it will have staying power even though it has within it unique aspects of that person's preferences, strengths, talents and potential.

6. THE ENCHANTED SELF TECHNIQUE: The technique consists of renaming and reframing positive components of one's past. The renaming and reframing is done through a review of one's history geared to separating dysfunction from function. The functional parts of one's past can then be valued for their positive components; properly labeled and/or put into a story line that allows the person to see her life history as meaningful in a positive way.

The reframing and renaming of components of one's past leads to clearer recognition of one's Positive Fingerprints of the Mind and/or Positive Shadows of the Mind. These now identified positive memories can be used to explore which positive aspects of one's self can be reincorporated so that one can experience ENCHANTED MOMENTS, THE ENCHANTED SELF and hopefully one's SONG OF THE SOUL.

7. THE SONG OF THE SOUL: A person's capacity to generate positive states of well-being repeatedly, reflecting that person's uniqueness in a multi-dimensional way, including preferences, talents, sense of purpose in life, commitment to others, values, relationship needs, etc. In order to sing one's SONG OF THE SOUL in one or many spheres of life, one must have developed sufficient self-esteem as well as the capacity know how to have one's needs met. THE SONG OF THE SOUL is a profound experience of THE ENCHANTED SELF.

8. RENAMING: Renaming is the act of pointing out to the client talents and other strengths that she may scarcely recognize as belonging to herself. She may have labeled them negatively, or she may not have recognized them at all.

9. REFRAMING: Reframing is a broader technique involving helping the client achieve a perceptual shift about herself by suggesting how her strengths can be woven into her life and her self-image. By suggesting a shift in the way she might view herself, your client has the opportunity to see her own life through new lenses as well as beginning the process of retelling her own story so that the

positive talents and strengths now recognized can emerge in a more prominent way. These strengths now take on meaning both in the present and in the past, giving value to painful times that prior to reframing had seemed pointless or negative.

10. THE HOLDING ENVIRONMENT: The Holding Environment is the safe haven that the therapist is able to establish with the client, so that the client feels regarded in a totally positive manner, but safe so that she can risk her inner self without the fear that she will be hurt. This is particularly important in terms of helping clients work on the positive aspects of themselves, because we make so little room for people to talk comfortably about what is right about themselves. People are often viewed as selfish or vain or narcissistic if they even attempt to validate their talents and their skills. This is particularly true for women, as documented in literature. Girls become less sure of their talents and less willing to develop them by adolescence.

11. SACRED SPACE: The term sacred space is used in this book to refer to an inner sense of wisdom that takes into account subtleties of privacy and the uniqueness of one's preferences and choices. When I talk about a person learning how to get her needs met, I am incorporating within that concept a sense of personal wisdom, the person knowing at some deep level what is right for her. Therefore, getting one's needs met takes into account a deep sensitivity to one's own sacredness, and, consequently the sacredness of others. If we don't encourage people to recognize their self-wisdom and their sense of sacred space, then they will orient themselves towards others' needs and expectations rather than to their own.

12. SELF-ESTEEM: As I define self-esteem I mean a person's capacity for appreciating and valuing the self. It assumes self-knowledge that contains within it wisdom and wonder so that the person can regard herself as unique and special within the context of the sacredness of all beings. (Thus, I do not only use this concept in terms of the psychological connotations of self-confidence and a sense of self-worth, although these notions are included.) I have broadened the concept of self-esteem to include an appreciation for the sacredness of one's self as well as that of others. Broadening the concept gives the therapist as well as the client more room to use

wisdom as one develops the capacity for THE ENCHANTED SELF.

13. SELF: In this book self is defined as the person's internalized awareness of being. "I think therefore I am." It is the perception of one's identity as a human being from deep inside the person, e.g., "I am a person with attributes, history and purpose."

References

1   Client's names and identities have been disguised.

2   Interviewees' names and identifying information have been disguised.

3   Paraphrased from Silent Prayer, Siddur for Friday Evening Services (San Francisco: Congregation Sha'ar Zahav).

4   Nancy McWilliams, "Psychodynamic Character Diagnosis as Differentiated from DSM-III-R Diagnosis – Individuality in Depth," Paper given at the New Jersey Psychological Fall Meetings, 1993.

5   Harville Hendrix, *Getting The Love You Want* (New York: Henry Holt, 1988).

6   M. S. Mahler, F. Pine and A. Bergman *The Psychological Birth of the Human Infant* (New York: Basic Books, 1975).

7   Charles L. Whitfield, *Healing The Child Within, Discovery and Recovery for Adult Children of Dysfunctional Families* (Deerfield, Florida: Health Communications, 1987).

8   Zelig Pliskin, *Begin Again Now: A Concise Encyclopedia of Strategies for Living* (New York: Gross Brothers Printing, 1993).

9   Marcel Proust, Quoted in a Greeting Card Illustrated by Mary Engelbreit (Bloomington, Indiana: Sunrise Publications, 1991).

10 Relatives' identities have been changed to protect the privacy of family members.

11   A Yiddish term meaning "a real person." Inside and outside, the person is the same. His/her ethical behaviors conform to his/her internal beliefs, which would be of high standards.

12   Gerta Lerner, *The Creation of Feminist Consciousness from the Middle Ages to 1870* (New York: Oxford University Press, 1994).

13   Sherry Ruth Anderson and Patricia Hopkins, *The Feminine Face of God* (New York: Bantam Book, 1991).

14   Joann Jackson Yelenik, "A Balabusta Coming Full Circle," *More of Our Lives*, edited by Sara Shapiro (Jerusalem, Israel: Targum Press, 1993).

15   Balabusta is a Yiddish expression for a homemaker with soul, who is a soul builder. She nourishes the insides of people who are in her domestic care as well as their physical bodies.

16   For ease in communication, I will refer to my clients as 'she' or 'her' unless otherwise specified. However, all the materials presented in this book are intended for universal use, for men, women and children.

17   Manis Friedman, *Doesn't Anyone Blush Anymore?* (San Francisco: Harper Collins, 1990).

18   Sheila Kongsberg, *Holy Days: The Life of a Hasidic Family* (New York: Collier Books, MacMillian, 1985).

19   Abraham S. Twerski, *Let Us Make Man* (New York: CIS Publishers, 1987).

20   A definition gathered from discussions with my Torah teacher.

21   *Diagnostic and Statistical Manual of Mental Disorders*, 3rd Edition (Washington, D.C.: The American Psychiatric Association, 1980).

22   Heocka SAFA, or Black Elk, born 1863 – from an unpublished collection or readings. Thanks to Barbara Fleisher, Ph.D.

23   Barbara Becker Holstein and Doreen Laperdon-Addison, "GROUP-WORK for Mental Health Providers Utilizing THE ENCHANTED SELF CONCEPT," *Groupwork*, Vol. 7(2), (1994), pp. 23–36.

24   I wish to thank my dear friend and colleague Dr. Sandra Prince-Embury who encouraged me to include this request. No matter how we look at the concept, it remains circular in its essence. Even in these last sentences I am requesting that we enter into a mutual endeavor.

Index